Pharmaceuticals in the European Union

Pharmaceuticals in the European Union:

Law and Economics

By

Giuditta Savonitto

Cambridge Scholars Publishing

Pharmaceuticals in the European Union: Law and Economics

By Giuditta Savonitto

This book first published 2019

Cambridge Scholars Publishing

Lady Stephenson Library, Newcastle upon Tyne, NE6 2PA, UK

British Library Cataloguing in Publication Data
A catalogue record for this book is available from the British Library

ISBN (10): 1-5275-3141-4
ISBN (13): 978-1-5275-3141-3

To young Italian trainee lawyers
exploited by old Italian lawyers.

TABLE OF CONTENTS

Part 2: Economics

LIST OF ILLUSTRATIONS

PREFACE

When approaching a topic that arouses personal interest, one of the biggest obstacles is finding the information needed to delineate the contours of the subject. In the study of classical and well-established subjects, this obstacle is overcome thanks to the handbooks that some venerable professor has drawn up by grouping together the fundamentals of that subject into one text. But often this facilitation does not exist.

As a matter of fact, it may happen that a scholar has to independently search for small fragments of information in order to construct, piece by piece, a general framework of the subject. In this way, it becomes necessary to wander among libraries, websites, databases, symposia, conferences and every vehicle of information to which the interested party has access.

It may also happen that, in the myriad of small pieces of information retrieved, there are conflicting data or opinions that, despite their initially negative impact, have the positive effect of developing a personal critical vision.

This is exactly what happened to the author of this modest book when she found herself writing the thesis of her Integrated Master of Arts in Law.

The subject matter of this interest is pharmaceuticals and, in particular, how and why the European Union regulates the safety of such products that constitute a fundamental element in everyone's life. The research was difficult and not without obstacles. First and foremost of these was finding the relevant information. Therefore, in a complex labyrinth of facts, laws, legal cases, legislative proposals, economic analyses, sector studies and requests to experts, the author has tried to reconstruct a matter that is nothing but a puzzle made up of many small pieces.

Putting together the tiles of the mosaic is the meaning of this book: providing the reader with a simple and general overview of what has been done and what can still be done at Union level to ensure the quality, safety and effectiveness of medicinal products while improving an equal patient access.

In the current political and social climate characterised by a growing wave of sovereignty and by the lack of confidence in science in which even principles that were assumed to be peaceful and assured are put in doubt, the strongest therapy against these "cancers" is precisely education. Informing the general population in a simple and clear way, even on technical and complex issues, must be one of the main objectives of the institutions. And which institutions can do it better than the European ones, which have the advantage of grouping together in a single great ideal the most diverse populations, geographically so close to each other and yet culturally so distant.

The reader of this book may be a pharmaceutical executive facing the complexity of regulatory rules and patient access in Europe as a whole and in the individual Member States. A journalist may find in these pages a wider frame in which to place particular news on a new therapy or a new EU regulation on medicines that he wants to share with his public. Members of institutions and governmental agencies may find here a summary of all the results obtained in this field over the past 50 years as well as a starting point to optimise the balance of public resources and medical opportunities. Additionally, health technology assessors may find here useful information for their complex analyses. This book is obviously also directed to lawyers, students and academic professors of law schools, as it provides an overview of the legislation, jurisprudence and governance that were created, amended and reformed by the legitimate European institutions with the aim to regulate the internal market and the safety of medicinal products in the Union. Finally, the author has tried to use a language that is as clear as possible for the curious layperson willing to make up his own mind about the opportunities for more efficient and wise healthcare delivery across Europe.

INTRODUCTION

More than 50 years ago, the first EU legislation on human medicines was enacted. From that time, the European Union has been one of the largest importers and exporters of medicinal products in the world.

The legal basis for the European legislator in the field of medicinal products is Article 168 of the Treaty on the Functioning of the European Union (TFEU), which stipulates that

> *(...) a high level of human health protection shall be ensured in the definition and implementation of all Union policies and activities.*

In particular, according to Article 168(4)(c), the European Parliament and the Council can adopt measures setting high standards of quality and safety for medicinal products to help Member States to achieve common safety standards, especially where domestic standards would otherwise prevent a high level of human health protection being achieved.

Indeed, the scope of action of the European legislator must follow the rule set by Article 4 TFEU, which, in its non-exhaustive list of the shared competences between the Union and the Member States, includes common safety concerns in public health matters, only allowing the EU's intervention when it can be useful to solve common problems related to the Union as a whole.

Despite this explicit but extremely limited legal basis for the regulation of medicines and, more generally, of healthcare[1], the EU has relied on different institutions and competences, especially those in the context of the single market program, in order to extend its influence in the healthcare matter.

---

[1] "Healthcare" here means the policy related to the organisational and financing aspects of healthcare provision and the treatments of individuals. See Mary Guy and Wolf Sauter, "The History and Scope of EU Health Law and Policy", in *Research Handbook on EU Health Law and Policy,* eds. Tamara K. Hervey, Calum Alasdair Young and Louise E. Bishop (Cheltenham: Edward Elgar Publishing, 2017), 21.

Thus, rather than a strong political ground, the Union's actions are based on the depoliticisation of the matter, the decisions of the Court of Justice of the European Union, a complicated institutional arrangement, the rules set by *ad hoc* created agencies and the numerous instruments of soft law[2] (such as the Open Method of Coordination[3]).

This situation has been conceptualised as a "patchwork" of health competences, characterised by different provisions belonging to different policy domains, some oriented to the market and others to social solidarity[4].

Health in the European Union is a complex policy in which there is a contradiction between the responsibility of the Member States in the organisation of their own healthcare systems and the European Union competence's in the creation and the development of the single market.

Further complicating this legal framework has been the discontinuous, uncertain and variable integrations of health policy in the 28 Member States[5].

As a matter of fact, health is an intricate matter that always faces a tension between economic and social priorities and balancing multiple policy interests. In this regard, there is a brilliantly theorised expression of "constitutional asymmetry" between the EU policies related to social protection and those related to market efficiency[6]: the EU has a huge regulatory role and strong enforcement powers in respect of the promotion of market efficiency, but weak competences and instruments for the development of social protection (and this, in particular, before the Lisbon Treaty[7] conferred the same legal value of the European Treaties to the Charter of Fundamental Rights of the European Union).

---

[2] "Soft law" here means quasi-legal instruments with no legally binding force or a weaker binding force with respect to the traditional legal instruments of hard law.

[3] Elias Mossialos et al., *Health Systems Governance in Europe: The Role of European Union Law and Policy* (New York: Cambridge University Press, 2010), 6.

[4] Tamara K. Hervey and Bart Vanhercke, "Health care and the EU: the law and policy patchwork", in *Health systems Governance in Europe: The Role of European Union Law and Policy,* eds. Elias Mossialos et al. (New York: Cambridge University Press, 2010), 84-133.

[5] Wolfram Lamping, "European Union Health Care Policy", in *European Union Public Health Policy – Regional and Global Trends*, eds. Scott L. Greer and Paulette Kurzer (New York: Routledge, 2013).

[6] Fritz W. Scharpf, "The European Social Model: Coping with Challenges of Diversity", *Journal of Common Market Studies* 40, no. 4 (December 2002): 645-670.

[7] The Lisbon Treaty was signed in 2007 and entered into force in 2009 after ratification by all the EU Member States.

As explained above, since the very beginning of the creation of the European Community, other areas of EU law have always had indirect effects in healthcare policies belonging to the competences of Member States. Thus, it was feared that the policies based on social solidarity would be overshadowed by liberal market-oriented policies[8]. In order to avoid such an interference and to safeguard their sovereignty, Member States have often appealed to the principle of subsidiarity[9] with respect to their pre-emption in healthcare, preventing, in this way, the firm inclusion of this matter in the European policy agenda[10]. Moreover, under the principle of proportionality, the Union's action content shall not exceed what is strictly necessary to achieve the objectives of the Treaties.

Despite the above-mentioned impediments, and especially because policy areas are difficult to keep fully separate, the European Commission indirectly expanded its role in the healthcare sector, mostly when healthcare relates to financial aspects and the free movement of goods, workers, services and capital.

In this way, among others, according to the free movement of workers, access to public healthcare systems for employees around the Union was coordinated, the European Health Insurance Card was created in order to facilitate emergency care abroad, and health professionals' diplomas obtained mutual recognition in all Member States. Similarly, by virtue of the free movement of goods, European regulations guarantee the safety and quality of pharmaceuticals and medical devices in the internal market[11].

But the "*biggest power shift since the single market was set up*" has been the growing EU involvement in national healthcare systems in the supervision of national budgets when Member States face fiscal stress,

---

[8] Mary Guy and Wolf Sauter, "The History and Scope of EU Health Law and Policy", CCP Working Paper 16-2 (Norwich: Centre for Competition Policy, University of East Anglia, 2016), 4, http://competitionpolicy.ac.uk/documents/8158338/11320618/CCP+WP+16-2+complete.pdf.

[9] The principle of subsidiarity seeks to safeguard the ability of Member States to take decisions in areas in which the EU does not have exclusive competence, and authorises intervention by the Union when the objective of an action cannot be achieved by the Member States. See Roberta Panizza, "The Principle of Subsidiarity", European Parliament, May 2018, http://www.europarl.europa.eu/ftu/pdf/en/FTU_1.2.2.pdf.

[10] Hans Vollaard, Hester Van de Bovenkamp and Dorte Sindbjerg Martisen, "The Making of a European Healthcare Union: A Federalist Perspective", *Journal of European Public Policy* 23, no. 2 (April 2016):157-176.

[11] Ibid., 9.

especially after the 2008 Eurozone financial crisis, and in particular for debt-struck countries[12]. The European Commission, in the context of the European Semester[13], formulated Country-Specific Recommendations (CSRs), which included general advice to curb health expenditure (for example through privatisation) and increase the cost-effectiveness of the healthcare system (especially by means of the generic substitution of medicines, better procurement, and e-health)[14].

Another important institutional subject, which has made a considerable contribution to the EU's involvement in healthcare matters, especially because of the lack of clarity and conflicts between the objectives of national policies and the European ones, is the Court of Justice of the European Union. The Court sets policy directions through the interpretation of very general legislative texts, basing most of its case law on the principles established in respect to free movement and antitrust laws. Indeed, the Court is seen as a driving force behind the health policy agenda in the light of the constitutional asymmetry[15].

The limited EU competence regarding healthcare gave importance to "new governance", a set of practices, such as networks, non-binding measures and guidelines, with a normative dimension but more distinct and softer than the rigid and formal mechanism of the traditional legal method.

Together, the European legislator, with its hard law[16], the Court, with its jurisprudence, and the new governance instruments implement the Union's healthcare policy through a hybrid mechanism of law and governance that mutually influence each other[17].

In this way, in spite of the national efforts to control health, EU institutions have managed to impact the national systems and strengthen

---

[12] Dave Keating, "The EU's Healthy Intervention", *European Voice*, October 4, 2013, https://www.politico.eu/article/the-eus-healthy-intervention/.

[13] The European Semester is an annual cycle of macro-economic, budgetary and structural policy coordination, which was approved by the Member States in 2010, after the economic crisis revealed the need for stronger economic governance at EU level. See: "European semester: a new architecture for the new EU Economic governance – Q&A", European Commission, last modified February 19, 2018, http://europa.eu/rapid/press-release_MEMO-11-14_en.htm.

[14] Guy and Sauter, "History", 29.

[15] Mossialos et al., *Health Systems Governance*, 10-18.

[16] "Hard law" here means the traditional normative tools created by authorities according to certain procedures, which produce binding rules.

[17] Hervey and Vanhercke, "Health care", 106.

the Union's integration, especially in relation to patients' and citizens' rights, the mutual recognition and improvement of the internal market and, more recently, the financial and budgetary field[18].

Apart from this necessary general introduction about EU healthcare policy, this book will be mostly focused on the European Union's patchwork and normative developments of pharmaceuticals regulation, a sector that has a direct impact on national healthcare policy and where the conflict between economic interests and social health considerations is quite incisive. Such a patchwork is characterised by two objectives pursued by the Union in its policy on pharmaceutical products: a high level of public health and innovation and, at the same time, a competitive industry.

The first objective, which is the health protection aspect in the application of Article 168 TFEU, is achieved through the controlled market access of only safe and effective medicines, the promotion of innovation, and a structured system that guarantees the supply of adequate information to patients.

The second objective, on the other hand, is the development and protection of a competitive European pharmaceutical industry, which especially ensures the free movement of medicinal products in the common market[19].

These two objectives are the common denominators of the entire European legal framework concerning medicinal products, which covers the whole lifecycle of pharmaceuticals.

The conflicting policies of the different stakeholders, the disparities between Member States, and the uncertainty created by the lack of a fully harmonised market prevent the creation of a single market for medicines[20].

In the last chapter of the book, the economic and social consequences of the market's fragmentation, caused by the national disparities in pharmaceuticals' pricing and reimbursement, will be analysed. Indeed,

---

[18] Guy and Sauter, "History", 31.

[19] Leigh Hancher, "The EU Pharmaceuticals Market: Parameters and Pathways", in *Health Systems Governance in Europe: The Role of European Union Law and Policy*, eds. Elias Mossialos et al. (New York: Cambridge University Press, 2010), 635-637.

[20] Govin Permanand and Christa Altenstetter, "The Politics of Pharmaceuticals in the European Union", in *Regulating Pharmaceuticals in Europe: Striving for Efficiency, Equity and Quality,* eds. Elias Mossialos, Monique Mrazek and Tom Walley (Maidenhead: Open University Press, 2004), 38.

there are many national health schemes within each European country and the pricing and reimbursement of pharmaceuticals are subject to very different rules across the Union. In particular, important inequalities in patient access to medicines exist between EU citizens. We will see that the main reasons for this problem can be of a double nature: first and foremost, the limited financial resources of middle-income Member States prevent the reimbursement of certain drugs to their citizens; second, the lack or inadequacy of the use of health technology assessments in order to decide which medicinal products, more or less cost-efficient, can efficiently be reimbursed or not.

Finally, the different techniques used by national regulators to establish the price of medicines, the mechanisms of cost containment applied to control public expenditure and the consequences of such price differentiations across the Union will be discussed.

The difficult achievement of a high level of human protection and equal patient access to medicines for all EU citizens is becoming even more arduous because of the financial crisis, the rising costs of health technologies, aging populations, and the higher incidence of some chronic diseases.

How will the Union address these growing problems?

In the current climate of mistrust towards European institutions and in a partially disaggregating Europe, will we still be able to talk about European Union health law in the future?

PART 1:

LAW

CHAPTER ONE

EUROPEAN UNION HARD LAW

1.1 The EU Legal Basis for Health

Over the past 50 years, the European legal basis for healthcare has been subject to a growing expansion. What has been witnessed has been a real enlargement of the competences conferred to the European institutions in this sector. Such a development has been explained not only in terms of the awareness that some public health problems are not manageable solely within national borders, but also as a compromise between those Member States that wanted further EU involvement in healthcare matters and those that, on the contrary, did not want any EU interference in their national health policy[21].

The original basis of the European integration was the creation of an internal market. As a consequence, the founding treaty of the European Economic Community (EEC), the Treaty of Rome[22] (1957), did not provide any explicit reference to health (with the exception of public health, as a justification for restrictions to free movement). Without such a positive provision and according to the principle of conferral[23], any policy areas not explicitly listed in the Treaties remain the Member States' competences. This situation has changed over time, and since the

[21] Tamara K. Hervey and Jean V. McHale, *Health law and the European Union* (Cambridge: Cambridge University Press, 2004), 69-73; Martin McKee, Elias Mossialos and Paul Belcher, "The Influence of European Law on National Health Policy", *Journal of European Social Policy* 6, no. 4 (November 1996): 263.

[22] Treaty establishing the European Economic Community, also known as the Treaty of Rome (adopted on March 25, 1957 and entered into force on January 1, 1958).

[23] The principle of conferral is a fundamental principle of EU law, laid down in Article 5 of the Treaty on European Union, according to which the EU acts only within the limits of the competences that EU countries have conferred upon it in the Treaties. Competences not conferred on the EU, and listed in Articles 2-6 of the TFEU, remain with the Member States.

beginning of the EEC, health issues have been brought under the market freedoms[24].

It was not until the Treaty of Maastricht[25] (1992) that the EU gained a punctual competence in the field of health, and in particular in the public health sector. In this regard, Article 129 specified the need for action in order to prevent illness and stipulated cooperation at the community level in order to ensure a high level of health protection.

Article 152 of the Treaty of Amsterdam[26] (1997) strengthened, in response to the BSE crisis[27], the need for cooperation in order to ensure that a high level of human health protection became an integral part of all the other European policies. This conferred upon the Directorate General for Health and Consumer Protection (DG SANCO)[28], an *ad hoc* created department of the EU Commission, the responsibility to protect and improve public health with a specific duty to conduct health impact assessments of EU policies. The same Article 152 established that

> *The action of Community in the field of public health shall respect precisely the responsibility of Member States in organizing and supplying health and medical assistance services*[29].

Subsequently, in 2000, the Charter of Fundamental Rights of the European Union[30] was adopted. It was used for the promotion of a rights-

---

[24] Guy and Sauter, "History and Scope", 19.

[25] Treaty on European Union, 1992 O.J. (C 191) 1. Now, the Consolidated version of the Treaty on European Union, 2012 O.J. (C 326) 13, https://eur-lex.europa.eu/legal-content/en/TXT/?uri=CELEX%3A12012M%2FTXT, (hereinafter TEU).

[26] Treaty of Amsterdam amending the Treaty on European Union, the Treaties establishing the European Communities and certain related acts-Final Act, 1997 O.J. (C 340) 115, https://eur-lex.europa.eu/legal-content/EN/TXT/?uri=CELEX %3A11997D%2FAFI.

[27] The Bovine Spongiform Encephalopathy (BSE), known as mad cow disease, which caused a crisis in 1996 when it was first diagnosed. "Bovine Spongiform Encephalopathy (BSE)", European Food Safety Authority, accessed November 3, 2018, https://www.efsa.europa.eu/en/topics/topic/bovine-spongiform-encephalopathy-bse.

[28] The DG SANCO changed its name to the Directorate-General for Health and Food Safety (DG SANTE) in 2015.

[29] Martin McKee, Tamara K. Hervey and Anna Gilmore, "Public Health Policies", in *Health Systems Governance in Europe: The Role of European Union Law and Policy*, eds. Elias Mossialos et al. (New York: Cambridge University Press, 2010), 235-237.

based approach in the field of EU health law[31]. This achievement was made possible especially thanks to provisions such as the rights to Services of General Economic Interest (Article 36), the integrity of the person (Article 3) and, notably, the right to healthcare enshrined in Article 35:

> *Everyone has the right of access to preventive health care and the right to benefit from medical treatment under the conditions established by national laws and practices. A high level of human health protection shall be ensured in the definition and implementation of all Union policies and activities.*

The current EU legal framework for health entered into force in 2009 with the Treaty of Lisbon[32], when Member States amended the two Treaties[33] which formed the constitutional basis of the European Union. Now, Article 168 TFEU, built on its predecessor, is the one referring to health. Compared to the previous Article 152 TEC, the Lisbon Treaty extended the scope of the EU's activities in the healthcare sector, but also introduced a stronger reference to Member States' responsibility for the definition of their health policies and the management of their health services.

Article 168 TFEU, reiterating that a high level of human health protection shall be ensured in the definition and implementation of all EU policies[34], confirms the impact of the above-mentioned dual nature of the competences of the Union in the field of health (as specified in Articles 4 and 6 TFEU), indicating the areas in which they can be performed through European institutions' acts. On the one hand, in accordance with Article 4 TFEU, and apparently in response to crises such as BSE and scandals like

---

[30] Charter of Fundamental Rights of the European Union, 2012 O.J. (C 326) 392, https://eur-lex.europa.eu/legal-content/EN/TXT/?uri=celex:12012P/TXT.

[31] Anniek de Ruijter, "A silent revolution: the expansion of EU power in the field of human health. A rights-based analysis of EU health law and policy" (PhD Thesis, University of Amsterdam, 2015).

[32] Treaty of Lisbon amending the Treaty on European Union and the Treaty establishing the European Community, 2007 O.J. (C 306) 1, https://eur-lex.europa.eu/legal-content/en/TXT/?uri=CELEX%3A12007L%2FTXT.

[33] The Treaty of Maastricht was updated in the Treaty on European Union (TEU), and the Treaty of Rome was updated in the Treaty on the Functioning of the European Union (TFEU).

[34] Consolidated version of the Treaty on the Functioning of the European Union, 2012 O.J. (C 202) 1, Article 168(1), https://eur-lex.europa.eu/legal-content/EN/TXT/?uri=celex%3A12012E%2FTXT (hereinafter TFEU).

HIV-infected blood[35], the EU may adopt harmonisation measures setting high standards of the quality and safety of human organs, blood, medicinal products and devices, and endorse protective measures in the veterinary field[36] only where domestic standards would otherwise prevent a high level of human health protection from being achieved. On the other hand, following the competences laid down in Article 6 TFEU, the EU may take, with ordinary legislative procedure, incentivising measures for the protection and improvement of human health, i.e. combating major cross-border health scourges, as well as acts regarding tobacco and alcohol in connection with the protection of public health, although excluding any harmonisation of national laws and regulations in these fields[37].

Cooperation between Member States is generally encouraged, but in particular with regard to the ultimate aim to improve the complementarity of national health services in cross-border areas. It is stated that

> *The Commission may, in close contact with the Member States, take any useful initiative to promote such coordination, in particular initiatives aiming at the establishment of guidelines and indicators, the organisation of exchange of best practice, and the preparation of the necessary elements for periodic monitoring and evaluation*[38].

Furthermore, the Council, on a proposal from the Commission, can adopt recommendations for the purposes set out in Article 168[39].

This framework has been linked to the use of different instruments of soft law by EU institutions and in particular to the Open Method of Coordination (OMC)[40].

The subsidiarity principle with regard to healthcare systems is reinforced in Article 168(7), which stipulates that the EU must respect the responsibilities of Member States for the definition of their health policy and the organisation, management and delivery of their health services, medical care and the allocation of the resources related to them.

Article 168(3) TFEU regulates an important aspect which reconfirms the EU's external competence rules[41]: the Union shall encourage cooperation

---

[35] Guy and Sauter, "History", 6.
[36] TFEU, Article 168(4).
[37] Ibid., Article 168(5).
[38] Ibid., Article 168(2).
[39] Ibid., Article 168(6).
[40] Guy and Sauter, "History", 13.

in the sphere of public health with third countries and the competent international organisations, especially the World Health Organisation (WHO).

Notwithstanding the explicit competence laid down in Article 168 TFEU, this is still not enough to outline a clear picture of the series of actions that the Union can put into place in order to protect public health. In this regard, Article 114 TFEU comes into play, which provides for the possibility of adopting harmonisation measures for the approximation of Member States' provisions that have as their object the establishing and functioning of the internal market[42]. It should be noted that most of the acts on public health have been adopted using this legal basis and not Article 168 TFEU. In this context, it is provided that the Commission, in proposing a measure concerning health,

> *(...) will take as a base a high level of protection, taking account in particular of any new development based on scientific facts*[43].

The prohibition laid down in Article 168(5) on the harmonisation of national laws directed to protect human health and the use of Article 114 TFEU as a legal basis for most EU health law has created tensions between the two provisions. Nevertheless, both of them have been used as the basis for the Tobacco Advertising[44] and the Patients' Rights[45] Directives[46].

In the judgments of the Tobacco Advertising I[47] and the Tobacco Advertising II[48] cases, in which Germany challenged the European Parliament and the Council, claiming that the Treaty provisions used as a

---

[41] Tamara K. Hervey, "EU Health Law", in *European Union Law,* eds. Catherine Barnard and Steve Peers (Oxford: Oxford University Press, 2014).
[42] TFEU, Article 114(1).
[43] Ibid., Article 114(3).
[44] The Tobacco Advertising Directive (2003/33/EC) bans cross-border tobacco advertising and sponsorship in the media, other than television, in all EU Member States.
[45] The Patients' Rights Directive (2011/24/EU) sets out the conditions under which a patient may travel across EU Member States in order to receive medical care and have the cost reimbursed by their own health insurance scheme.
[46] Guy and Sauter, "History", 7.
[47] Case C-376/98, Federal Republic of Germany v. European Parliament and Council of the European Union, 2000 E.C.R. I-08419, ECLI:EU:C:2000:544.
[48] Case C-380/03, Germany v. European Parliament and Council of the European Union, 2006 E.C.R. I-11573, ECLI:EU:2006:772.

legal basis for the Tobacco Advertising Directive were inappropriate, the Court of Justice clarified the relationship between the two Treaty provisions. The Court specified that Article 114 TFEU is the appropriate legal basis when there are differences between Member States' provisions, which have a direct effect on the functioning of the internal market because they obstruct the four fundamental freedoms.

Moreover, the harmonisation prohibition of Article 168(5) does not mean that harmonising measures adopted on the basis of other provisions of the Treaty cannot have any impact on the protection of human health[49].

Furthermore, so long as the conditions for recourse to Article 114 TFEU as a legal basis are fulfilled, the Community legislator cannot be prevented from relying on that legal basis on the grounds that public health protection is a decisive factor in the choices to be made[50]. This means that the European legislator cannot create laws within health as a single objective, but there must be an internal market connection as a legal basis[51].

Lastly, the Court stressed the connection with public health protection with reference to Article 168(1) TFEU, which provides that a high level of human health protection must form a constituent part of the other Community's policies, and Article 114(3) TFEU, which requires that, in achieving harmonisation, a high level of protection of human health should be ensured[52].

All of this is reflected in the main objectives of the EU legislation on medical products which are, on the one hand, the protection of public health in respect of Article 168 TFEU and, on the other, the improvement and application of the free movement of medical products in the EU in accordance with Article 114 TFEU.

---

[49] Case C-376/98, *Federal Republic*, para 78.
[50] Ibid., para 88.
[51] Anniek de Ruijter, "*The Impediment of Health Laws. Values in the Constitutional Setting of the EU*", in *Research Handbook on EU Health Law and Policy,* eds. Tamara K. Hervey, Calum Alasdair Young and Louise E. Bishop (Cheltenham: Edward Elgar Publishing, 2017).
[52] Case C-376/98, *Federal Republic*, para 88.

1.2 The Developments of EU Legislation on Pharmaceuticals

The first Community rules on pharmaceuticals were introduced, more than 50 years ago, in the wake of one of the darkest episodes in European pharmaceutical history: the thalidomide tragedy.

In the post-World War II era, sleeplessness was a common problem for many people, resulting in a high demand for tranquilisers all over Europe and, in particular, for thalidomide, the only non-barbiturate sedative known at the time.

A West German pharmaceutical company developed thalidomide as an anticonvulsive drug in the 1950s. On the basis of the producer's safety claims, the apparently harmless thalidomide was licensed in 1956 for prescription-free over-the-counter sale in Germany and most European countries. Furthermore, some medical doctors, after it was discovered that the drug also alleviated morning sickness, started recommending this off-label use of the drug to pregnant women, setting a worldwide trend[53].

In 1961, it was discovered that thalidomide has disastrous side effects: it interfered with the babies' normal development, creating nerve damage in the limbs and thus causing phocomelia. By March 1962, the drug was banned in most of the countries where it had previously been sold[54]. Nevertheless, in little more than a decade, over 10,000 children were born with thalidomide-related disabilities worldwide[55].

The thalidomide disaster showed the need for evidence-based authorisation of medicinal products before being placed on the market in order to test and ensure their safety. The European Economic Community legislator, as it then was, decided to develop structured medicinal

[53] Bara Fintel, Athena T. Samaras, Edson Carias, "The Thalidomide Tragedy: Lessons for Drugs Safety and Regulation", *Helix Magazine*, June 28, 2009. https://helix.northwestern.edu/article/thalidomide-tragedy-lessons-drug-safety-and-regulation.

[54] Despite its harmful side effects, thalidomide is approved for two uses today: the treatment of inflammation associated with Hansen's disease and as a chemotherapeutic agent for patients with multiple myeloma.

[55] James H. Kim and Anthony R. Scialli, "Thalidomide: The Tragedy of Birth Defects and the Effective Treatment of Disease", *Toxicological Sciences* 122, no. 1 (February 2011): 1-6.

regulations, and so in January 1965, the first Directive (Council Directive 65/65/EEC[56]) on pharmaceuticals was introduced.

It is worth noting that this Directive, like most of the subsequent ones, was based on Article 114 TFEU in referring to the internal market, which legitimated the European institutions to harmonise their national legislation in order to create and develop the free movement of medicinal products. Indeed, in the preamble, it is specified that the Directive was adopted because

> *(...) trade in proprietary medicinal products within the Community is hindered by disparities between certain national provisions, in particular between provisions relating to medicinal products (...) [and since] such disparities directly affect the establishment and functioning of the common market (...) such hindrances must accordingly be removed [giving priority to the removal of] the disparities liable to have the greatest effect on the functioning of the common market.*

The excellence of this Directive was that, as shown in its preamble, it defined the policy that still characterises the current EU regulation on medicines: to safeguard public health without hindering the development of the pharmaceutical industry or internal market trade.

The above-mentioned European pharmaceutical Directive was a first rudimentary effort to harmonise communitarian legislation and progressively eliminate the national differences in the field of medicinal products[57], especially with regard to their marketing authorisation and labelling[58].

Another aspect of the innovation of this Directive was the definition of medicinal products established in Article 1. It specified a list of a range of substances including a variety of biological products derived from human, animal, vegetable and chemical sources[59], which was updated only 30

---

[56] Council Directive 65/65/EEC of 26 January 1965 on the approximation of provisions laid down by Law, Regulation or Administrative Action relating to proprietary medicinal products, 1965 O.J. 22 369, https://eur-lex.europa.eu/eli/dir/1965/65/oj.

[57] Alexander Von Schwerun, Heiko Stoff and Bettina Wahrig, *Biologics, a history of agents made from living organisms in the twentieth century* (London: Routledge, 2015), 18.

[58] Article 1, Directive 65/65/EEC defines proprietary medicinal products as "*any ready-prepared medicinal product placed on the market under a special name and in a special pack*".

[59] Schwerun, Stoff and Wahrig, *Biologics*, 18.

years later when the EMEA established a Biologics Working Party (BWP)[60].

The salient features of the authorisation system at that time can be summarised as follows. According to Articles 3 and 4 of the Directive, the person responsible for placing a medicinal product on the market had to request an application, accompanied by specific particulars and documents listed in Article 4, to be made to the national competent authority in order to start the authorisation procedure which had to be completed within 120 days[61].

The competent authorities of Member States could refuse[62], suspend or revoke[63] the marketing authorisation when: the product proved to be harmful in the normal conditions of use; its therapeutic efficacy was lacking; its qualitative and quantitative composition was not as declared in the application; or the specific provisions about the labelling were not observed[64].

Once the authorisation was obtained, it had a validity of five years and could be extended for further five-year periods[65].

It was not until 1975 that the provisions laid down in Directive 65/65/EEC were amended and their implementation further ensured through additional requirements and procedures.

The second Council Directive 75/319/EEC[66] was adopted in order to continue the approximation of national laws and regulations related to proprietary medicinal products and, secondly, to foster the progress towards the free movement of such products across the Community market. For these purposes, a Committee for Proprietary Medicinal Products was set up[67], consisting of Member States' representatives and

---

[60] The Biologics Working Party (BWP) was established to provide recommendations to the EMEA scientific committees on all matters relating directly or indirectly to quality and safety aspects relating to biological and biotechnological medicinal products.

[61] Directive 65/65/EEC, Article 7.

[62] Ibid., Articles 5 and 6.

[63] Ibid., Article 11.

[64] Ibid., Article 20.

[65] Ibid., Article 10.

[66] Second Council Directive 75/319/EEC of 20 May 1975 on the approximation of provisions laid down by law, regulation or administrative action relating to proprietary medicinal products, 1975 O.J. (L 147) 13, http://data.europa.eu/eli/dir/1975/319/oj.

[67] The Committee for Medicinal Products for Human Use (CHMP) replaced the former Committee for Proprietary Medicinal Products (CPMP) in May 2004.

the Commission, responsible for giving opinions on the compliance of a medicine with the requirements set out in Directive 65/65/EEC and for facilitating the adoption of a common position regarding marketing authorisation by the Member States[68].

Directive 75/319/EEC represented the first step towards a joint EU position on marketing authorisation through a multistate licensing procedure. Indeed, it introduced the mutual recognition of Community countries of their respective national authorisations, with the aim of bringing innovative pharmaceuticals to patients across Europe.

As a matter of fact, according to Article 9, if the responsible person requested the forwarding of a specific authorisation to at least five other Member States, the Member State which had issued such an authorisation had to forward it to the Committee which, for its part, had to advance the dossier to the competent authorities of the Member States so specified. Notably,

> *(...) such forwarding shall be deemed to be equivalent to submitting an application for marketing authorisation, within the meaning of Article 4 of Directive 65/65/EEC, to the said authorities[69].*

Moreover, the Directive stated that Member States should take all appropriate measures to ensure that the documents and particulars for the marketing authorisation request, before their submission to the competent authorities, should be drawn up by experts with the necessary technical or professional qualifications.

The last innovational aspect covered by the Directive which is worth remembering is the control, at a national level, of goods imported from third countries, and, in particular, with regard to holding marketing authorisation.

In the same year, the Standards and Protocol Directive 75/318/EEC[70] was adopted. It defined the tests to be carried out both on the raw materials, during all the stages of production, and on the finished medicinal products, to be presented by the respective manufacturers.

---

[68] Directive 75/319/EEC, Article 8(1).

[69] Directive 75/319/EEC, Article 9(3).

[70] Council Directive 75/318/EEC of 20 May 1975 on the approximation of the laws of Member States relating to analytical, pharmaco-toxicological and clinical standards and protocols in respect of the testing of proprietary medicinal products, 1975 O.J. (L 147) 1, http://data.europa.eu/eli/dir/1975/318/oj.

The Directive also covered indications for running clinical trials. It was stated that the evaluation of the application for marketing authorisation had to be based on clinical pharmacological experiments expressly designed to determine the therapeutic efficacy and safety of the product under normal conditions of use, and that the therapeutic advantages had to outweigh the potential risks.

All these provisions were of great importance in all the countries of the European Community because they allowed, on the one hand, the applicants to know precisely which data were required for registration and, on the other, the national competent authorities to receive the same data and reach the same assessment[71].

Despite the first hint of mutual recognition of marketing authorisations introduced by Directive 75/319/EEC, the path towards a greater simplification of the procedure was still long and treacherous.

In 1983, with Directive 83/570/EEC[72], Member States agreed on a uniform way to summarise the key characteristics of an authorised product. The Directive consisted of the amendments and supplements introduced in Directives 65/65/EEC, 75/318/EEC and 75/319/EEC, agreed after a series of discussions at Community level, especially on the mutual recognition of national licenses.

In the preamble, it is specified that if a marketing authorisation for a medicinal product has been given in one Member State on the basis of harmonised provisions, this medicine would be also allowed in another Member State, taking the initial authorisation into due consideration[73].

An important innovation introduced with this Directive is the binding nature of the Summary of Product Characteristics (SPC) to be submitted by the applicant and approved by the national competent authorities before any medicinal product is authorised[74]. The SPC is the most important

---

[71] C. Steichele, V. Abshagen and J. Koch-Weser, *Drugs between Research and Regulations: Proceedings of the 5th International Meeting of Pharmaceutical Physicians Munich* (Berlin: Springer-Verlag Berlin Heidelberg, 2013), 166-168.

[72] Council Directive 83/570/EEC of 26 October 1983 amending Directives 65/65/EEC, 75/318/EEC and 75/319/EEC on the approximation of provisions laid down by law, regulation or administrative action relating to proprietary medicinal products, 1983 O.J. (L 332) 1, http://data.europa.eu/eli/dir/1983/570/oj.

[73] Steichele, Abshagen and Koch-Weser, *Drugs,* 166-168.

[74] Now the SPC must be completed and submitted as an application to the European Medicines Agency, the European Chemicals Agency or one of the national competent authorities of the Member States before marketing is authorised.

public document consisting of the definitive description of a product resulting from the summary of the data on its efficacy, safety and quality. Moreover, the product can be marketed for the approved indications only. The aim of such a document is to give information on how the product is to be used for a specific treatment and, more importantly, it is binding on the pharmaceutical industry in all of its promotional and marketing activities for any single specific medicinal product[75].

The thalidomide disaster, besides highlighting the demand for pharmaceutical safety and quality tests, also showed the need to create rules for the compensation for victims and the desire to embrace a set of harmonised private law rules on strict liability posed by products[76]. Such an appeal was met with the adoption of the Product Liability Directive[77] (PLD) in 1985, which is still in force. Among the main purposes of the Directive, consumer protection, repeatedly mentioned in the Recitals, is one of the most important and is guaranteed through a system of liability that is defect-based and not fault-based[78]. The PLD applies to all products, as broadly defined by Article 2:

(...) all movables even if incorporated into another movable,

hence, surely even to medicines. Under the Directive, liability lies with the producer of the defective product, expansively defined in Article 3 also

---

[75] Jose Luis Valverde and Paul Weissenberg, *The Challenges of the New EU Pharmaceutical Legislation* (Amsterdam: IOS Press, 2005), 60-61.

[76] Marcus Pilgerstorfer, "EU Law and Policy on Pharmaceuticals Marketing and Post-market Control Including Product Liability", in *Research Handbook on EU Health Law and Policy,* eds. Tamara K. Hervey, Calum Alasdair Young and Louise E. Bishop (Cheltenham: Edward Elgar Publishing, 2017), 172.

[77] Council Directive 85/374/EEC of 25 July 1985 on the approximation of the laws, regulations and administrative provisions of the Member States concerning liability for defective products, 1985 O.J. (L 210) 29, http://data.europa.eu/eli/dir/1985/374/oj.

[78] Liability without fault was chosen as 'the sole means of adequately solving the problem, peculiar to our age of increasing technicality, of a fair apportionment of the risks inherent in modern technical production". Recital 2 PLD. See also Case C-300/95, Commission v. United Kingdom, 1997 E.C.R. I-02649, ECLI:EU: C:1997:255, Opinion of the AG, para 16; Case C-402/03, Skov Æg v. Bilka Lavprisvarehus A/S and Bilka Lavprisvarehus A/S v. Jette Mikkelsen and Michael Due Nielsen, 2006 E.C.R. I-00199, ECLI:EU:C:2006:6, para 19.

to include quasi-producers[79], any importer in the EU market and any supplier if the producer cannot be identified. In addition to the producer, in the context of pharmaceuticals, a marketing authorisation holder may also be considered liable for the damages caused by a specific medicinal product.

In order to gain a compensation for harms, according to Article 4, the injured person must prove that the product was defective, that he suffered a recoverable damage and that there was a causal link between these two. If the person satisfies this burden, the onus shifts onto the producer, who, for his part, can protect himself by proving one of the defences listed in Article 7 or that the consumer's negligence caused or contributed to the damage. As provided for by Article 7, the producer shall not be liable if he proves that he did not put the product into circulation; or the defect did not exist at that time; or the product was neither manufactured nor distributed by him; or the defect is due to the compliance of the product with mandatory regulations; or scientific knowledge was not enough to enable the recognition of the defect's existence; or, in the case of a manufacturer of a component, that the defect is attributable to the design of the product or to the instructions given by the manufacturer of the product.

In general, and to conclude this quick clarification on product liability, the strict product liability rules across all Member States can nowadays be described as harmonised[80].

In 1987, the Council adopted two more Directives on pharmaceuticals.

The first one[81], Directive 87/21/EEC, adapting the provisions of the original Directive 65/65/EEC to consider scientific progress and operational experience, defined rules for copies of branded medicines, the so-called generics, without affecting the industrial and commercial property of the innovative industries.

A generic medicine contains the same active substance(s) of an already authorised medicinal product, and it is used in the same dose(s) to treat the

---

[79] Defined in Article 3, Product Liability Directive, as: "*any person who, by putting his/her name, trade mark or other distinguishing feature on the product, presents himself/herself as the producer*".

[80] Pilgerstorfer, "EU Law", 172-182.

[81] Council Directive 87/21/EEC of 22 December 1986 amending Directive 65/65/EEC on the approximation of provisions laid down by law, regulation or administrative action relating to proprietary medicinal products; 1987 O.J. (L 15) 36, http://data.europa.eu/eli/dir/1987/21/oj.

same disease(s)[82]. For these reasons, according to Article 1, an applicant should not be required to provide the results of the pharmacological tests or the clinical trials if he demonstrated that the medicinal product was essentially similar and intended for the same therapeutic use as the corresponding branded one, and that the person responsible for the original medicine had consented to the clinical references or that the medicinal product had a well established medicinal use.

The second Council Directive on medicines adopted in 1987[83] introduced the Concertation Procedure, a Community mechanism conceived in order to arrive at uniform decisions on high-technology medicinal products throughout the different Member States. According to this mechanism, the relevant national competent authorities, before taking a decision on a marketing authorisation, could ask a simple licensing opinion of an EU level committee, the Committee for Proprietary Medicinal Products or the Committee for Veterinary Medicinal Products, in accordance with their competence, for all new high technology medicinal products.

Compared to the previously established multistate licensing procedure[84], this new mechanism (the precursor of the current centralised procedure) fostered cooperation between national drug regulatory authorities, partly because the scientific expertise available to each of them was not always sufficient to resolve problems posed by these highly technically advanced products. However, each Member State remained solely responsible for granting the marketing authorisation, and, most importantly, both procedures were still based on voluntary cooperation[85].

In 1989, the Council adopted two more Directives in order to extend the scope of the previous Directives (65/65/EEC and 75/319/EEC) to specific types of medicinal products: vaccines, toxins, serums, and

[82] However, a generic medicine's inactive ingredients, name, appearance and packaging can be different. See "Generic and hybrid medicines", European Medicines Agency, accessed November 10, 2018, http://www.ema.europa.eu/ema/index.jsp?curl=pages/special_topics/document_listing/document_listing_000335.jsp&mid=WC0b01ac0580514d5c.

[83] Council Directive 87/22/EEC of 22 December 1986 on the approximation of national measures relating to the placing on the market of high-technology medicinal products, particularly those derived from biotechnology; 1987 O.J. (L 15) 38, http://data.europa.eu/eli/dir/1987/22/oj.

[84] Introduced by Directive 75/319/EEC.

[85] Pierre-Louis Lezotre, *International Cooperation, Convergence and Harmonization of Pharmaceutical Regulations: A Global Perspective* (Oxford: Academic Press, 2013), 83-84.

allergens[86] and to medicinal products derived from human blood or human plasma[87].

Also in 1989, the first guidelines on Good Manufacturing Practices (GMP) for medicinal products were published to improve the quality of medicines throughout the European Community. Moreover, all Member States agreed that the GMP requirements of medicinal products for human use, specified in Directive 91/356/EEC [88], were also applicable to veterinary medicinal products, as shown by Directive 91/412/EEC[89].

The GMP is a code describing the minimum standard that any pharmaceutical manufacturer must comply with in order to ensure that the requirements of the marketing or clinical trial authorisation are met, and that the products are of a high quality and appropriate for their intended use [90]. Although the guidelines of the GMP, which are documents providing guidance on the scientific or regulatory aspects of the development of medicines, are not legally binding, the applicants need to provide justification for any deviations.

From their introduction until today, the Commission has always revised GMP guidelines in order to take scientific advances and the

---

[86] Council Directive 89/342/EEC of 3 May 1989 extending the scope of Directives 65/65/EEC and 75/319/EEC and laying down additional provisions for immunological medicinal products consisting of vaccines, toxins or serums and allergens; 1989 O.J. (L 142) 14, http://data.europa.eu/eli/dir/1989/342/oj.

[87] Council Directive 89/381/EEC of 14 June 1989 extending the scope of Directives 65/65/EEC and 75/319/EEC on the approximation of provisions laid down by Law, Regulation or Administrative Action relating to proprietary medicinal products and laying down special provisions for medicinal products derived from human blood or human plasma; 1989 O.J. (L 181) 44, http://data.europa.eu/eli/dir/1989/381/oj.

[88] Commission Directive 91/356/EEC of 13 June 1991 laying down the principles and guidelines of good manufacturing practice for medicinal products for human use; 1991 O.J. (L 193) 30, http://data.europa.eu/eli/dir/1991/356/oj.

[89] Commission Directive 91/412/EEC of 23 July 1991 laying down the principles and guidelines of good manufacturing practice for veterinary medicinal products; 1991 O.J. (L 228) 70, http://data.europa.eu/eli/dir/1991/412/oj.

[90] "Good manufacturing practice", European Medicines Agency, accessed November 13, 2018 http://www.ema.europa.eu/ema/index.jsp?curl=pages/regulation/general/general_content_001205.jsp&mid=WC0b01ac0580027088.

continual improvement of best practices in the field of quality into account, in collaboration with the European Medicines Agency[91].

The relevant market for each medicinal product was, and still is, *de facto* national because their pricing remains the Member States' competence. The wide differences in the pharmaceuticals' pricing cause the so-called parallel imports of medicines from one EU country, in which they are cheaper, to another, in which they are more expensive, in order to profit from the price difference. The European institutions claim that parallel imports of pharmaceuticals foster competition between Member States, leading to a reduction in the prices of medicines.

Member States with more expensive pharmaceutical prices have tried to prevent such parallel imports, thus hindering the free movement of goods in the internal market, often using the protection of intellectual property rights as a justification. But the Court of Justice of the European Union has consistently legitimated such measures, arguing that they serve the secure financial stability of national health systems[92]. At the same time, the Court has called for more transparency in pharmaceutical pricing in order to check that such rules do not constitute unlawful protectionist discrimination against medicinal products from other Member States[93]. Therefore, consolidating this case law, the so-called Transparency of Pharmaceuticals Pricing Directive[94] was adopted in 1989. This legislative text imposed a series of procedural requirements, such as a public annual list of medicine prices or a specific timeframe within which decisions must be taken, designed to verify that national pricing and reimbursement decisions do not create obstacles to the EU pharmaceutical trade. The Directive provisions did not affect national policies on the setting of prices, nevertheless it did not achieve its objectives and Member States have regularly infringed the procedural obligations imposed by it[95]. For

[91] "EudraLex-Volume 4-Good Manufacturing Practice (GMP) guidelines", European Commission, accessed November 14, 2018, http://ec.europa.eu/health/documents/eudralex/vol-4/index_en.htm.
[92] see: e.g. Case C-181/82, Roussel Laboratoria BV and others v. État néerlandais, 1983 E.C.R. 03849, EU:C:1983:352; Case C-249/88, Commission of the European Communities v. Kingdom of Belgium, 1991 E.C.R. I-01275, EU:C:1991:121.
[93] Tamara K. Hervey and Jean V. McHale, *European Union Health Law: Themes and Implications* (Cambridge: Cambridge University Press, 2015), 270.
[94] Council Directive 89/105/EEC of 21 December 1988 relating to the transparency of measures regulating the prices of medicinal products for human use and their inclusion in the scope of national health insurance systems; 1989 O.J. (L 40) 8, http://data.europa.eu/eli/dir/1989/105/oj.
[95] Hervey and McHale, *European Union Health Law*, 271.

this reason, in 2012, the European Commission proposed a new Transparency Directive[96] with a view to simplifying and increasing respect for this legislation while maintaining the original unchanged aims. The proposal, amended the following year, was ultimately withdrawn because, after 16 meetings of the Working Party on Pharmaceuticals and Medical Devices, no agreement was foreseeable in the Council, where objections had been made by a number of EU Member States[97].

At a meeting held in Brussels in April 1990, the international cooperation in the field of pharmaceutical regulation was further enhanced with the International Conference on Harmonisation of Technical Requirements for Registration of Pharmaceuticals for Human Use (ICH). Now, all the relevant EU law on medicines operates in the context of the ICH.

Gathering the regulatory authorities of Japan, United States, and Europe, together with experts from the pharmaceutical industry, the ICH is an international platform where technical aspects concerning drug registration can be discussed. Since its inception, it has worked to ensure worldwide harmonisation for the quality, safety and efficacy of medicinal products with the further purpose to achieve greater harmonisation in the interpretation and application of technical guidelines and requirements for the products' registration. The underlying thought of the ICH is that harmonisation would optimise the economical use of resources, speeding up global development and the availability of new medicines due to the avoidance of duplication of efforts in the testing needed for new pharmaceuticals and the consequent delay to bring such new products to the market[98].

---

[96] European Commission, *Proposal for a Directive of the European Parliament and of the Council relating to the transparency of measures regulating the prices of medicinal products for human use and their inclusion in the scope of public health insurance systems*, COM (2012) 84 final. Amended by: European Commission, *Amended proposal for a Directive of the European Parliament and of the Council relating to the transparency of measures regulating the prices of medicinal products for human use and their inclusion in the scope of public health insurance systems*, COM (2013) 168 final.

[97] The formal withdrawal of the proposal was published on March 7, 2015 O.J. (C 80) 17. See "Transparency Directive", European Commission, accessed November 28, 2018, https://ec.europa.eu/growth/sectors/healthcare/competitiveness/products-pricing-reimbursement/transparency-directive_it.

[98] Hervey and McHale, *European Union Health Law,* 324.

In the light of the safeguarding of public health, when the Maastricht Treaty created the European Union in 1992, a series of Directives were adopted to further establish the EU internal market and consequently facilitate the free movement of medicinal products around the twelve Member States of that time.

In particular, those Directives harmonised: the wholesale distribution of medicines, with the aim of exercising control over its entire chain so as to guarantee that such products are stored, transported and handled in suitable conditions (Directive 92/25/EEC[99]); the classification for the supply of medicines (Directive 92/26/EEC[100]); the labelling of pharmaceuticals in order that medicinal products could be used correctly on the basis of full and comprehensible information, providing a high degree of consumer protection (Directive 92/27/EEC[101]); and the principles governing the advertising of medicines (Directive 92/28/EEC[102]).

Finally, during the same year, via the adoption of Directive 92/73/EEC[103], the scope of the harmonisation of laws and regulations concerning medicines was extended to homeopathic products.

Despite all the efforts, laws, conferences, and guidelines made by the European institutions since the first Community pharmaceutical regulation in 1965, the resulting development of a single market in medicinal products was insufficient and unsatisfactory[104]. For this reason, an

---

[99] Council Directive 92/25/EEC of 31 March 1992 on the wholesale distribution of medicinal products for human use; 1992 O.J. (L 113) 1, http://data.europa.eu/eli/dir/1992/25/oj.

[100] Council Directive 92/26/EEC of 31 March 1992 concerning the classification for the supply of medicinal products for human use; 1992 O.J. (L 113) 5, http://data.europa.eu/eli/dir/1992/26/oj.

[101] Council Directive 92/27/EEC of 31 March 1992 on the labelling of medicinal products for human use and on package leaflets; 1992 O.J. (L 113) 8, http://data.europa.eu/eli/dir/1992/27/oj.

[102] Council Directive 92/28/EEC of 31 March 1992 on the advertising of medicinal products for human use; 1992 O.J. (L 113) 13 http://data.europa.eu/eli/dir/1992/28/oj.

[103] Council Directive 92/73/EEC of 22 September 1992 widening the scope of Directives 65/65/EEC and 75/319/EEC on the approximation of provisions laid down by Law, Regulation or Administrative Action relating to medicinal products and laying down additional provisions on homeopathic medicinal products; 1992 O.J. (L 297) 8, http://data.europa.eu/eli/dir/1992/73/oj.

[104] Lezotre, *International Cooperation*, 84.

agreement on a centralised, EU-wide procedure was reached for the authorisation of human and veterinary medicinal products.

This new European pharmaceutical system was created by two major texts.

The first one, Directive 93/39/EEC [105], introduced the Mutual Recognition Procedure (MRP), reforming and facilitating the multistate licensing one. This new type of procedure, which applies today to the majority of conventional medicinal products, is based on the principle of the recognition of a pre-existing national marketing authorisation by one or more Member States (the details on how the MRP works will be specified in the next section).

The second legislative text, adopted in 1993, Regulation (EEC) No. 2309/93 [106], was enacted with the aim of improving the marketing authorisation of medicinal products. It represented a strong political decision because it created, through the additional incorporation of the CPMP, the European Agency for the Evaluation of Medicinal Products (EMEA) [107], a decentralised agency responsible for the scientific evaluation, supervision and safety monitoring of medicines throughout the Union.

Moreover, the Centralised Procedure was also introduced, which is still in place today, and which, by replacing the Concertation Procedure, allows applicants to submit a single application to the EMEA in order to obtain a marketing authorisation for a medicinal product which will then be valid throughout the entire EU (see the next section for details)

In 1995, the EMEA started business and came into operation, and in the same year the first centralised marketing authorisation was granted by the European Commission.

The surveillance of medicinal products on a national level includes the post-marketing investigation by the Official Medicines Control Laboratories

---

[105] Council Directive 93/39/EEC of 14 June 1993 amending Directives 65/65/EEC, 75/318/EEC and 75/319/EEC in respect of medicinal products; 1993 O.J. (L 214) 22, http://data.europa.eu/eli/dir/1993/39/oj.

[106] Council Regulation (EEC) No. 2309/93 of 22 July 1993 laying down Community procedures for the authorisation and supervision of medicinal products for human and veterinary use and establishing a European Agency for the Evaluation of Medicinal Products; 1993 O.J. (L 214) 1, https://ec.europa.eu/health/sites/health/files/files/eudralex/vol-1/reg_1993_2309/reg_1993_2309_en.pdf.

[107] The EMEA was renamed the European Medicines Agency (EMA) in 2004.

(OMCLs). In general, after the manufacturing pharmaceutical company has carried out a quality release investigation on the medicines, the different OMCLs, through post-marketing laboratory random sample testing, determine if medicinal products meet the conditions as specified in their approval. Among the various competences of the OMCLs, besides the mere examination of medicines' quality and safety, that must be remembered are the tasks to monitor whether the labelling is in accordance with legal requirements, to study those suspected of counterfeiting medicines and, lastly, to verify the correctness of the analytical methods used by the manufacturers.

In 1994, in order to save public money through collaboration in resource pooling and as a useful means for the avoidance of the duplication of efforts of national competent authorities' work, the Commission of the European Union and the Council of Europe decided to create a network of OMCLs, joined by the European Directorate for the Quality of Medicines (EDQM), which would be responsible for the coordination of technical activities. This international collaboration also contributed to the spread of harmonised common standards.

Since the beginning of the new millennium, the European legislator has turned his attention to orphan medicinal products[108] for the main purpose of increasing the number of products for rare diseases.

Indeed, the pharmaceutical industry and public authorities have been historically disinclined to advance the scientific research and development of medicines to treat these rare diseases since, due to the high costs and a consequent tiny pool of users, it was not economically convenient to produce such medicines. In response, the EU introduced new strong legislation, Regulation (EC) No. 141/2000[109], which provides incentives for the research, marketing and development of orphan medicines as well as the enactment of a centralised procedure for their appointment.

To date, the European Commission has already authorised 141 orphan medicines and designated 1,495 products as orphan medicinal products. In this way, companies with an orphan designation for a medicinal product benefit from incentives such as a 10-year market exclusivity period post authorisation for designated products, fee waivers, assistance for

---

[108] Orphan medicinal products are intended for the diagnosis, prevention or treatment of life-threatening or very serious conditions that affect no more than 5 in 10,000 people in the European Union.

[109] Regulation (EC) No. 141/2000 of the European Parliament and of the Council of 16 December 1999 on orphan medicinal products; 2000 O.J. (L 18) 1, http://data.europa.eu/eli/reg/2000/141/oj.

marketing authorisations, and the possibility of a Community marketing authorisation.

Regulation (EC) No. 141/2000 also created a specialised decision-making committee at the EMEA, the Committee for Orphan Medicinal Products (COMP), responsible for recommending and evaluating applications for orphan designation. The most important innovation introduced with the COMP was the inclusion, for the first time in European pharmaceutical regulation history, of patient representatives as full members of a scientific committee. This has increased the transparency of the EMEA's decision-making process and, at the same time, has encouraged dialogue with patient groups.

In 2000, as established in Article 71 of Regulation (EEC) No. 2309/93, the Commission published the first general report summarising all the experience acquired by the new system implemented in 1995. This report analysed the relationship between the results obtained over the first five years and the prefixed objectives (namely the creation of a single market in medicinal products and a high level of health protection). The audit showed that the centralised procedure has performed its role with notable success and that the EMEA was considered a very important means in the achievement of a harmonised European Community pharmaceutical market. For such reasons, it was felt that: the centralised procedure should be opened up to a broader range of products; a real supervisory between Member States was necessary to earn a greater application of the mutual recognition principle; and that there was a demand to decrease the administrative burden where public health implications were absent.

These critical points were particularly felt especially in the light of the upcoming major enlargement of the EU (in 2004, ten more additional countries became EU Member States), which would stress the weaknesses of the system if such issues were not removed by then[110].

In order to simplify the complexity of the European pharmaceutical legislation, the EU Parliament and the Council conducted a comprehensive review of its legislation in the pharmaceutical sector with the adoption of Directive 2001/83/EC[111], the so-called "Community Code Directive". This codification brought together all previous Directives in one single text (except for the legal provisions provided by Regulation (EEC) No.

[110] Lezotre, *International Cooperation,* 85-86.

[111] Directive 2001/83/EC of the European Parliament and of the Council of 6 November 2001 on the community code relating to medicinal products for human use; 2001 O.J. (L 311) 67, http://data.europa.eu/eli/dir/2001/83/oj.

2309/93) and, in particular, it considered the disparities between certain national provisions directly affecting the functioning of the EU internal market. Therefore, it represented an important reformation, especially because all the previous legislation adopted since 1965 had been frequently amended, creating, in this way, great confusion and reducing the simplicity of the legislation necessary for a better achievement of legal certainty.

Another important factor introduced by the Community Code Directive was the extension of the list of medicines subjected to the marketing authorisation. Indeed, the Directive is said to be a provision of "*exhaustive harmonisation*" because it is applicable to the vast majority of medicines marketed in the European Union. The only excluded pharmaceuticals from its scope, according to Article 3, are products prepared in pharmacies for individual patients and advanced therapy medicinal products to be used under the control of specific professionals and prepared for specific patients on a non-routine basis[112].

As a result, at that time, there remained two main pieces of legislation regulating pharmaceuticals: Regulation (EEC) No. 2309/93, dealing with products subject to the centralised authorisation procedure, and the Community Code Directive, which applied to all medicinal products to be authorised by a national authorisation or mutual recognition procedure.

This latter Directive, constantly amended in the following years, is still the basis of the current pharmaceutical legislation concerning the regulation of drugs in the EU and the framework for the regulation of medicines at a national level.

Also in 2001, the Directive 2001/20/EC[113] was adopted. Also known as the "Clinical Trials Directive", it was the first step towards the approximation of different types of legislation for the implementation of good clinical practice in the conduct of clinical trials[114] on medicinal products.

---

[112] Hervey and McHale, *European Union Health Law,* 326.

[113] Directive 2001/20/EC of the European Parliament and of the Council of 4 April 2001 on the approximation of the laws, regulations and administrative provisions of the member states relating to the implementation of good clinical practice in the conduct of clinical trials on medicinal products for human use; 2001 O.J. (L 121) 34, http://data.europa.eu/eli/dir/2001/20/oj.

[114] Clinical trials, as defined by the European legislator, are investigations on humans intended to discover or verify the effects of one or more investigational medicinal products ("IMPs"). See "Clinical trials – General information", European Commission, accessed November 28, 2018,

It is important to remember that the provisions established by this legislation were inspired by the ethical principles for clinical research adopted for the first time with the Declaration of Helsinki[115] (DoH) in 1964, which have been revised seven times to date. Among the fundamental principles established by the Declaration we find respect for the individual (Article 8) and the right to informed consent[116] before any human being participates in clinical trials (Articles 20, 21 and 22).

As explicitly stated in the Directive recitals, Member States' requirements for carrying out clinical trials diverged broadly, causing delays and confusion that were detrimental to trials' effective conduct in the Community. For this reason, it was felt necessary to simplify and harmonise the related provisions by establishing a clear, transparent procedure and improve the effective coordination of such clinical trials at EU level[117]. The Directive covered the protection of the clinical trials' subjects, the ethics committee, the commencement and conduct of the trials, the exchange of information, infringements, the manufacture and import of investigational medicinal products, the notification of serious adverse reactions, clinical trials on minors and adults incapable of giving informed legal consent.

Without getting into details about how clinical trials must be conducted (this will be explained in the next section, dedicated to the current functioning of the European regulatory system of medicines), it is worth noting that, in order to approve the involvement of human subjects in such trials, the verification of the clinical trial's compliance with the standards of good clinical practice is crucial,[118] especially for ensuring the credibility of the related date.

---

https://ec.europa.eu/health/human-use/clinical-trials/information_en.

[115] World Medical Association, *Declaration of Helsinki – ethical principles for medical research involving human subjects*, June 1964, https://www.wma.net/policies-post/wma-declaration-of-helsinki-ethical-principles-for-medical-research-involving-human-subjects/.

[116] According to Article 2, Directive 2001/20/EC, Informed Consent is "*the decision, which must be written, dated and signed, to take part in a clinical trial, taken freely after being duly informed of its nature, significance, implications and risks and appropriately documented, by any person capable of giving consent or, where the person is not capable of giving consent, by his or her legal representative; if the person concerned is unable to write, oral consent in the presence of at least one witness may be given in exceptional cases, as provided for in national legislation*".

[117] Directive 2001/20/EC, Recital 10.

[118] The EMA defines Good Clinical Practice (GCP) as "*an international ethical and scientific quality standard for designing, recording and reporting trials that*

With the aim of improving a harmonised and coordinated standard system for clinical trials around the European Community, all the relevant information on the content of a clinical trial should be made accessible to all Member States. For this reason, a European database [119] bringing together all the above-mentioned information, with due regard for the rules of confidentiality, has been set up.

The European legislator also found it was essential to monitor adverse reactions using Community surveillance (pharmacovigilance) procedures in order to ensure the immediate cessation of any clinical trial with an unacceptable level of risk[120].

Three years later, for the sake of clarity, another major legislative impact occurred with the adoption of Regulation (EC) No. 726/2004[121], which replaced Regulation (EEC) No. 2309/93. This reform was a consequence of the above-mentioned Commission report on the experience acquired as a result of the procedures laid down in Regulation (EEC) No. 2309/93. From the conclusions of that report, it emerged that it was imperative to improve the operation of the marketing authorisation procedures and to amend certain administrative aspects of the European Agency for the Evaluation of Medicinal Products (the name of this agency changed to the European Medicines Agency[122], especially in the light of scientific developments and the upcoming enlargement of the European Union.

While always trying to guarantee high standards in the quality and safety of medicines and including measures to encourage competiveness, the Regulation also reinforced the monitoring procedures. As such, Member States must inform the EMA and the Commission when the manufacturer fails to fulfil their obligations under an authorisation. Moreover, the holder of a marketing authorisation must notify any

---

involve the participation of human subjects"; see "Good-clinical-practice compliance", European Medicines Agency, accessed November 28, 2018, http://www.ema.europa.eu/ema/index.jsp?curl=pages/regulation/general/general_content_000072.jsp.

[119] "The EU Clinical Trials Register", European Medicines Agency, accessed November 28, 2018, https://www.clinicaltrialsregister.eu/about.html.

[120] Directive 2001/20/EC, Recital 18.

[121] Regulation (EC) No. 726/2004 of the European Parliament and of the Council of 31 March 2004 laying down Community procedures for the authorisation and supervision of medicinal products for human and veterinary use and establishing a European Medicines Agency; 2004 O.J. (L 136) 1, http://data.europa.eu/eli/reg/2004/726/oj.

[122] Regulation No. 726/2004, Recital 2.

variation or suspension of a medicinal product to the Commission and the EMA, which, for this reason, administers the EudraVigilance database, collecting all the monitored and reported information.

In order to maintain a high level of scientific evaluation and preserve its relative confidence in patients and healthcare professionals, the compulsory purview of the centralised authorisation's procedure was expanded to include orphan medicines, products derived from biotechnology, advanced therapy pharmaceuticals (i.e. based on the manipulation of genes, cells or tissues) and products containing any new substance to treat acquired immune deficiency syndrome (AIDS), cancer, neurodegenerative disorder, diabetes, or other viral diseases.

Another noteworthy innovation introduced by the Regulation in question was the enlargement of the EMA's competences and responsibilities, such as creating a database on medicinal products accessible to the general public, assisting EU countries with communication with healthcare professionals, and coordinating the evaluation and monitoring systems of medicinal products.

From 2004 to the present day, this Regulation, amended several times, together with Directive 2001/83/EC represent the two pillars of European pharmaceutical legislation.

In the same year, EU competent institutions agreed that the rules on pharmaceutical products for human use should also be applied to traditional herbal medicines[123].

For this reason, and in order to simplify the registration procedure, Directive 2004/24/EC was introduced[124]. Such simplified registration procedures, intended for herbal medicines with a long tradition and which do not fulfil the requirements for a marketing authorisation, sought to eliminate the national divergences about their status and also to facilitate, with the introduction of harmonised rules, the free movement of such products in the EU internal market. In particular, the applicant only had to prove, with detailed references to published scientific literature from at

[123] Herbal medicinal products, as defined by the European Commission, are "as any medicinal product, exclusively containing as active ingredients one or more herbal substances, one or more herbal preparations, or a combination of the two"; See "Herbal medicinal products", European Commission, accessed November 21, 2018, https://ec.europa.eu/health/human-use/herbal-medicines_en.

[124] Directive 2004/24/EC of the European Parliament and of the Council of 31 March 2004 amending, as regards traditional herbal medicinal products, Directive 2001/83/EC on the Community code relating to medicinal products for human use; 2004 O.J. (L 136) 85, http://data.europa.eu/eli/dir/2004/24/oj.

least the previous 30 years, that the constituent of a product has a well-established medicinal use with accepted efficacy and safety.

Of great importance was the creation of a Committee for Herbal Medicinal Products (HMPC) at the EMA, composed of scientific experts in the field, tasked with the setting of the Community monographs for traditional herbal medicinal products. With a view to further facilitating registration, the HMPC was also assigned the duty to arrange a draft list of herbal substances considered safe under normal conditions of use because they have been in medicinal use for a long time.

The latest noteworthy innovation, which occurred in 2004, was the introduction of EU rules for copies of biological products ("biosimilars") with Directive 2004/27/EC[125].

The EU was the first institution to create a legal framework and a regulatory pathway for "*similar biological medicinal products*"[126] and, for this reason, it inspired many countries around the world. Moreover, over the past 10 years, the EU has authorised the highest number of biosimilars worldwide, collecting a lot of experience in relation to their use, approval and safety[127].

The European Commission is responsible for the release of the authorisation, valid in all EU Member States, of these particular medicines on the basis of the scientific opinions provided by the EMA and according to the same standards of all biological medicinal products. In order to avoid the repetition of clinical trials already carried out, applicants have to demonstrate through comprehensive comparability studies with the 'reference' biological pharmaceutical that their biological medicine is highly similar to the reference one, especially in terms of safety, quality and efficacy.

---

[125] Directive 2004/27/EC of the European Parliament and of the Council of 31 March 2004 amending Directive 2001/83/EC on the Community code relating to medicinal products for human use; 2004 O.J. (L 136) 34, http://data.europa.eu/eli/dir/2004/27/oj.

[126] Similar biological medicinal products, commonly called "biosimilars", are biological medicines that are very similar to another already approved biological medicine (the "reference medicine") containing active substances from a biological source; see "Biosimilar medicines", European Medicines Agency, accessed November 22, 2018, http://www.ema.europa.eu/ema/index.jsp?curl=pages/medicines/general/general_content_001832.jsp.

[127] "*Biosimilars in the EU. Information guide for healthcare professionals*", EMA and European Commission, last updated on April 27, 2017, http://www.ema.europa.eu/docs/en_GB/document_library/Leaflet/2017/05/WC500226648.pdf.

All of these innovations taken as a whole further demonstrate the consistency of the European legislator in pursuing its prefixed objectives, in particular with regard to the harmonisation and development of the internal market of medicinal products, always guaranteeing high standards of safety, quality and health protection without hindering the pharmaceutical industry market with unnecessary bureaucratic and administrative duplications.

Two years later, in December 2006, the Union adopted specific legislation on medicinal products for children: the so-called Paediatric Regulation[128].

The aim of this Regulation, which considerably changed the system for paediatric medicine in Europe, was to improve the health of children, aged 0 to 17 years, by promoting the accessibility of particular medicines dedicated to them without redundant trials or delaying the authorisation of pharmaceuticals for adults' use. Indeed, this legislative text is structured around three main objectives: more medicines for children, better product information, and more paediatric research.

For the achievement of these purposes, a series of obligations directed to the pharmaceutical industries have been established, such as the screening of every new product for its potential use on children, but also rewards and incentives to encourage the research and development of medicines for children's specific therapeutic needs.

The legislator also decided to dedicate a specific committee, the Paediatric Committee (PDCO), replacing the previous Paediatric Working Group, to coordinate the EMA's work on medicines for children, but especially to regulate the studies that companies must perform on children as part of their Paediatric Investigation Plans (PIPs)[129]. PIPs must be included in all applications for the marketing authorisation of a new medicine and must be approved by the EMA.

---

[128] Regulation (EC) No. 1901/2006 of the European Parliament and of the Council of 12 December 2006 on medicinal products for paediatric use and amending Regulation (EEC) No. 1768/92, Directive 2001/20/EC, Directive 2001/83/EC and Regulation (EC) No. 726/2004; 2006 O.J. (L 378) 1, http://data.europa.eu/eli/reg/2006/1901/oj.

[129] Paediatric Investigation Plans (PIPs) are defined by the EMA as "*development plan[s] aimed at ensuring that the necessary data are obtained through studies in children, to support the authorisation of a medicine for children*"; see "Paediatric investigation plans", European Medicines Agency, accessed November 28, 2018, http://www.ema.europa.eu/ema/index.jsp?curl=pages/regulation/general/general_content_000608.jsp&.

Since its entry into force in 2007, the Commission, once a year, publishes and makes available on its website a report on companies and products that have benefited from incentives, as well as companies that have failed to comply with the above-mentioned obligations.

In 2007, the first Regulation (Reg. (EC) 1394/2007[130]) on Advanced Therapy Medicinal Products (ATMPs) was introduced, which contains their overall framework. For the sake of clarity, ATMPs are new medical products, the precursors of revolutionary medical treatments, based on genes, cells, and tissues.

The introduction of this Regulation was felt to be necessary because the divergent national approaches on advanced therapies prevented patient access to products, impeded the growth and competitiveness of the pharmaceutical industry, and hindered the high level of health protection required to be guaranteed in the Union.

For these reasons, the Regulation: introduced the centralised procedure for such medicines; created, within the EMA, the Committee for Advanced Therapies (CAT) in order to assess advanced therapy products; specified technical requirements; and provided incentives for small and medium-sized companies, the most involved economic operators in this field.

Three years later, the EU pharmacovigilance rules were reviewed to refine and improve the system for medicines' safety through better prevention, detection and assessment of Adverse Drug Reactions (ADRs).

The main reason for which pharmacovigilance was created was ADRs. Indeed, despite medicines' safety and quality being ensured by controls and repeated clinical trials being conducted before a marketing authorisation is granted, the EMA estimated that unintended responses and rare side effects to medicine caused around 197,000 deaths per year in Europe alone[131].

---

[130] Regulation (EC) No. 1394/2007 of the European Parliament and of the Council of 13 November 2007 on advanced therapy medicinal products and amending Directive 2001/83/EC and Regulation (EC) No. 726/2004; 2007 O.J. (L 324) 121, http://data.europa.eu/eli/reg/2007/1394/oj.

[131] "Legal Framework", European Medicines Agency, accessed November 23, 2018, http://www.ema.europa.eu/ema/index.jsp?curl=pages/special_topics/general/general_content_000491.jsp.

Hence, two different legislative texts were approved (Regulation (EU) No. 1235/2010[132] and Directive 2010/84/EU[133]) in order to reduce the number of ADRs through the better collection of data, rapid assessment and effective regulatory action of issues related to the safety of medicines, direct reports, greater transparency and the improvement of EU decision-making procedures in this field.

In this way, the pharmacovigilance system monitors the development of already authorised medicines and allows the national competent authorities to be notified of any adverse drug reactions, including through a direct report made by the patients.

By systematically collecting the data on each authorised medicine and taking the necessary precautions, the competent authorities can protect public health from the risks arising from the use of any medicines, and, in this way, ensuring their safety. Therefore, to minimise all the potential risks associated with the use of any medicine, the legislative texts in question introduced a system of proactive and proportionate risk management directed under the responsibility of an *ad hoc* created committee: the Pharmacovigilance Risk Assessment Committee (PRAC), established at the EMA.

An example of how the European legislator usually incorporates the principles enshrined by the CJEU in its judgments is Directive 2011/24/EU[134], which sets out the conditions under which an EU citizen may travel to receive medical care across the Union. Indeed, the Directive, commonly known as the Patients' Rights Directive, specifies that it is

---

[132] Regulation (EU) No. 1235/2010 of the European Parliament and of the Council of 15 December 2010 amending, as regards pharmacovigilance of medicinal products for human use, Regulation (EC) No. 726/2004 laying down Community procedures for the authorisation and supervision of medicinal products for human and veterinary use and establishing a European Medicines Agency, and Regulation (EC) No. 1394/2007 on advanced therapy medicinal products; 2010 O.J. (L 348) 1, http://data.europa.eu/eli/reg/2010/1235/oj.

[133] Directive 2010/84/EU of the European Parliament and of the Council of 15 December 2010 amending, as regards pharmacovigilance, Directive 2001/83/EC on the Community code relating to medicinal products for human use; 2010 O.J. (L 348) 74, http://data.europa.eu/eli/dir/2010/84/oj.

[134] Directive 2011/24/EU of the European Parliament and of the Council of 9 March 2011 on the application of patients' rights in cross-border healthcare; 2011 O.J. (L 88) 45, http://data.europa.eu/eli/dir/2011/24/oj.

(...) intended to achieve a more general, and also effective, application of principles developed by the Court of Justice[135] *on a case-by-case basis*[136].

In particular, such legislation implements the principle that

(...) the Treaty provisions on the freedom to provide services include the freedom for the recipients to healthcare, including persons in need of medical treatment, to go to another Member State in order to receive it there[137].

Thus, patients travelling to another EU country to receive medical care will enjoy equal treatment as accorded to the citizens of the country in which they are treated. Moreover, if the travelling person is entitled to the same healthcare service at home, then he has the right to reimbursement by his own national health system.

But what is important to note for the purpose of this work, and in particular for the discussion that will follow in Chapter Four, is the call for strong cooperation between European countries in health technology assessments through the creation of a voluntary network. Such cooperation in the evaluation of new health technologies and the subsequent exchange of information can support Member States through economies of scale; a better evidence base for the optimal use of new technologies; and the reduction of the duplication of efforts.

In October 2012, the 2010 legislation was further improved because of some pharmacovigilance incidents. In point of fact, during the two intervening years, EMA found that the risks caused by an anorectic agent, benfluorex, were greater that the relative benefits. For this reason, all medicines containing this agent were revoked throughout the European market. This issue was addressed by Directive 2012/26/EU [138] and

[135] See, for example, Case C-120/95, Nicolas Decker v. Caisse de maladie des employés privés, 1998 E.C.R. I-01831, ECLI:EU:C:1998:167; Case C-158/96, Raymond Kohll v. Union des caisses de maladie, 1998 E.C.R. I-01931, ECLI:EU:C:1998:171.

[136] Directive 2011/24/EU, recital 8.

[137] Ibid., recital 26.

[138] Directive 2012/26/EU of the European Parliament and of the Council of 25 October 2012 amending Directive 2001/83/EC as regards pharmacovigilance; 2012 O.J. (L 299) 1, http://data.europa.eu/eli/dir/2012/26/oj.

Regulation (EU) No. 1027/2012[139], which have further consolidated the health protection of patients.

Furthermore, in the same year, the Commission introduced a black symbol to identify medicinal products that are subject to additional monitoring in order to encourage patients to report ADRs seen in the use of these pharmaceuticals through national reporting systems.

Another piece of legislation that should be mentioned, although it does not properly affect pharmaceuticals but certainly has an impact on their development in pre-clinical testing, is Directive 2010/63/EU[140] on the protection of animals used for scientific purposes. The provisions laid down are firmly based on the principle of the three Rs: replace, reduce and refine the use of laboratory guilds and seek to harmonise the variety of animals' welfare standards across the Union. Moreover, the development of alternative methods to animal experimentation is promoted.

In 2011, the European legislator was concerned about regulating a problem that, due to increasingly developed falsification techniques, reaches more and more patients in the EU every year and, for this reason, still poses a serious threat to public health: falsified medicines.

Falsified medicines are fake medicines that pass themselves off as authorised ones, and therefore lack quality, safety and efficacy. Hence, in order to prevent the entering into the market of such medicinal products, the Falsified Medicines Directive (Directive 2011/62/EU[141]) was adopted.

To this end, new measures were included: compulsory safety features on pharmaceuticals' packaging; a common Union logo that identifies legal online pharmacies; stricter rules on the inspections of producers of active medicinal ingredients; and more record-keeping requirements for distributors.

---

[139] Regulation (EU) No. 1027/2012 of the European Parliament and of the Council of 25 October 2012 amending Regulation (EC) No. 726/2004 as regards pharmacovigilance; 2012 O.J. (L 316) 38, http://data.europa.eu/eli/reg/2012/1027/oj.

[140] Directive 2010/63/EU of the European Parliament and of the Council of 22 September 2010 on the protection of animals used for scientific purposes; 2010 O.J. (L 276) 33, http://data.europa.eu/eli/dir/2010/63/oj.

[141] Directive 2011/62/EU of the European Parliament and of the Council of 8 June 2011 amending Directive 2001/83/EC on the Community code relating to medicinal products for human use, as regards the prevention of the entry into the legal supply chain of falsified medicinal products; 2011 O.J. L (174) 74, http://data.europa.eu/eli/dir/2011/62/oj.

The most important obligation that this Directive imposed on Member States is the prevention of the market circulation of medicines suspected of being falsified. For this purpose, the Commission may define, in a delegated act, the criteria and details to be verified in the assessment of the potentially falsified character of those products.

Member States must also ensure that national manufacturers of active substances comply with their respective good manufacturing practices in accordance with the principles and guidelines set up by the Commission.

Moreover, in Article 46b(2) of this Directive, EU-wide rules for the importation of active substances are specified: they can only be imported after the competent authority of the exporting third country has confirmed in writing that the standards of the GMP and control of the active substances in question are equivalent to those of the Union.

As mentioned just before, the Falsified Medicine Directive introduced a "common logo" that legally-operating online pharmacies must display on all their website pages. This logo ensures that the medicine being sold by a legally authorised pharmacy, and which therefore is included in the official national lists, meets the official standards for safety, quality and efficacy.

The Commission had the remit to establish, *inter alia*, the design and technical requirements of the common logo that became compulsory on 1 July 2015. However, it is up to the Member States to determine the specific conditions for the retail supply of medicinal products to the public.

Figure 1-1 The EU-wide common logo for identifying legal online pharmacies[142] (See centrefold for this image in colour)

[142] Data source: "EU logo for online safe of medicines", European Commission, accessed November 28, 2018, https://ec.europa.eu/health/human-use/eu-logo_en.

In pursuing the traditional aim of greater cross-border cooperation, and in the search for greater administrative simplification and practicality, in 2014, the new Clinical Trials Regulation[143] was adopted.

In the light of the problems raised in the application of Directive 2001/20/EC, the need for such a review was widely recognised, particularly in regard to: the differences in the implementations across Member States; the excessive levels of bureaucracy; the uncertain time intervals required for authorisations; and the multiple submissions for trials involving more than one country[144].

Without going into details about the process of conducting clinical trials (a topic that will be discussed in the next section), let us now look at the major innovations that this new legislation brought.

First of all, since it is a Regulation, and like all European Union Regulations is directly applicable in the legal system of the Member States, it therefore does not need to be implemented through an *ad hoc* created domestic law. In any case, according to Article 99, all its provisions should not be applied earlier than 28 May 2016 and, until that moment, the previous Directive continued to be in force. After that date, a transition period lasting three years started: during the first year, clinical trials could be submitted under both the 2001 Directive and the 2014 Regulation systems; however, during the second and third years, trials authorised under the previous system remained under it. Finally, at the end of this transitional period, all the clinical trials would be conducted following the new rules.

The objectives of this new legislative text are: the protection of the clinical trials' subjects; the reliability of the relative generated data; the promotion of innovation; the simplification of the clinical trials' application process (in particular for multi-country trials); and the intensification of transparency.

The European legislator, in creating the measures necessary to attain these objectives, has always sought to maintain a balance between the need to protect public health and the fostering of innovations in medical research without forgetting about the economic interests of the sponsors. It is clear that behind these more sectorial goals that can also be found in the

---

143 Regulation (EU) No. 536/2014 of the European Parliament and of the Council of 16 April 2014 on clinical trials on medicinal products for human use, and repealing Directive 2001/20/EC; 2014 O.J. (L 158) 1, http://data.europa.eu/eli/reg/2014/536/oj.

144 Carlo Petrini, "Regulation (EU) No. 536/2014 on clinical trials on medicinal products for human use: an overview", *Annali dell'Istituto Superiore di Sanità* 50, no. 4 (2014): 317-321, http://old.iss.it/publ/anna/2014/4/504317.pdf.

previous Clinical Trials Directive, the Regulation in question has the overall objective of making the European Union more attractive for Research and Development (R&D).

For this reason, a single authorisation valid for all Member States was introduced, as well as a single portal and a database containing all data from clinical trials performed throughout the EU.

Although some operational aspects have yet to be perfected, which is presumably when the Regulation will become fully applicable, detailed procedures for the submission, assessment and evaluation of requests for the authorisation of clinical trials have been defined.

The noteworthy key changes introduced with respect to the previous Directive can be summarised as follows: a single e-submission to all Member States concerned via an EU portal; coordinated assessment; one single decision per Member State; a risk adapted approach for those trials conducted with already authorised medicines; the reinforced supervision of clinical trials by a Union Control in Member States; the concept of co-sponsorship; new provisions for informed consent; and a damage compensation system to be set up by the Member States.

To conclude, even though some of the novelties established by this long and complex Regulation (composed of 99 articles plus 7 annexes), details of which will be outlined in the next section, have yet to be refined, a lot of criticisms and perplexities have already been outlined by operators and stakeholders.

The latest law that is worth recalling in this brief analysis and historical reconstruction of European legislative developments on medicinal products is the new Regulation (EU) No. 2017/745[145] on medical devices.

Firstly, it is necessary to make a clarification. Despite the fact that medical devices and pharmaceuticals are both essential to healthcare, EU law has treated them quite separately due to the important differences between the two. Devices are essentially mechanical in nature, whereas pharmaceuticals are chemical and intended to actively influence the body's metabolic system, leading to greater potential health risks. Medical devices range from simple products such as dentures or disposable gloves to extremely advanced equipment such as pacemakers or coronary stents. The technologies used for these devices extend far beyond those of

---

[145] Regulation (EU) 2017/745 of the European Parliament and of the Council of 5 April 2017 on medical devices, amending Directive 2001/83/EC, Regulation (EC) No. 178/2002 and Regulation (EC) No. 1223/2009 and repealing Council Directives 90/385/EEC and 93/42/EEC; 2017 O.J. (L 117) 1, http://data.europa.eu/eli/reg/2017/745/oj.

pharmaceutical science and include bioengineering, engineering, electronics, software and others, and thus there are big differences in the respective research and development models.

Despite these dissimilarities and the distinctiveness of each regulatory framework, medical devices and medicines share similarities[146]. First of all, they have the same constitutional legal basis with the consequent weak European Union competencies in matters concerning public health. Hence, the objectives of their regulations are the promotion of the internal market through the enhancement of the European industry's competitiveness and, above all, the protection of public health through meeting safety, quality and efficacy requirements.

Medical devices' legislation has primarily specified the essential requirements that such devices must fulfil in order to be placed on the market with a special product safety certification; the procedure for the assessment of conformity; and the conditions for clinical investigation and labelling.

The new Regulation (EU) No. 2017/745, which will supposedly come into force in 2020, is intended to guarantee greater oversight of certification bodies; impose stricter *ex-ante* control for high-risk devices via new pre-market scrutiny; ensure more effective post-market surveillance and traceability of devices; reinforce the rules on clinical evidence; and improve the coordination mechanisms between EU Member States in the fields of vigilance and market surveillance.

In this way, the legislator has applied a very similar approach to that concerning European law on pharmaceuticals, thus bringing the two legal frameworks closer together[147].

1.3 The EU Regulatory System for Pharmaceuticals

In the previous section, a rapid analysis of the regulatory developments that the European legislator has adopted and implemented in the field of medicinal products has been conducted.

It has been seen that, since 1965, through directives, regulations, conferences and guidelines, the competent European institutions have tried to guarantee a high level of quality, safety and efficacy of medicines,

---

[146] Christa Altenstetter, *Medical devices: European Union policymaking and the implementation of health and patient safety in France* (New Brunswick, N.J.: Transaction Publishers, 2008), chapter 3.

[147] Catherine Barnard and Steve Peers, *European Union Law* (Oxford: Oxford University Press, 2017), 647-648.

favouring the free movement of such products in the internal market, and, at the same time, creating a fertile ground for scientific research and technological discoveries without hindering one of the major stakeholder's interests in this field, namely the pharmaceutical industry.

In this way, through numerous reforms and amendments, the current regulatory system of medicines has been created.

In this section, the individual aspects of the long journey to the supervision of the medicines' safety, from clinical trials to pharmacovigilance, will be discussed in order to understand how the system operates.

This entire overview will also be necessary to understand which particular aspects of medicines' regulation remain the Member States' competence, with the further aim of introducing and better comprehending the discussion that will be undertaken in Chapter Four in relation to the consequences that the non-harmonisation at a European level of some of these aspects implies.

Pharmaceutical products are regulated at almost all stages of their life-cycle and beyond. The current EU law supervises medicinal products as defined by Article 1 Directive 2001/83/EC in two alternative and broadly-interpreted[148] criteria:

> *(a) Any substance or combination of substances presented as having properties for treating or preventing disease in human beings; or*
> *(b) Any substance or combination of substances which may be used in or administered to human beings either with a view to restoring, correcting or modifying physiological functions by exerting a pharmacological, immunological or metabolic action, or to making a medical diagnosis.*

Behind this body of law, a confused blend of *ratio legis* and policy concerns, often conflicting, can be observed. The most difficult policies to balance are certainly those that seek, on the one hand, to enhance consumer protection and drug safety, and, on the other hand, to foster an

---

[148] See (for example): Case 35/85, Procurer de la République v. Gérard Tissier, 1986 E.C.R. 01207, ECLI:EU:C:1986:143, para 26, "*the definition of medicinal product[s] (...) may not be interpreted restrictively but must be construed as including substances which are not administered as they are to human beings or animals but which are manufactured separately and are intended to be used mixed with other substances, either as a simple combination of substances or after chemical transformation, or as a carrier substance*".

environment conducive to medical research, technological innovation and industrial development[149].

These policies have, *inter alia*, the purpose of solving the biggest and most imminent problems afflicting this sector, namely the growing aging of the population and the ever-increasing healthcare costs.

For the attainment of these goals, the legislator has created and developed a series of instruments which guarantee that a medicinal product fulfils the legal requirements in terms of quality, safety and efficacy, consequently implying the increase in access to cost-effective medicines, the minimisation of health risks, the reduction of drug overutilisation[150], the improvement of transparency, greater harmonisation, and the greater trust of patients in pharmaceuticals and healthcare professionals.

Among the principles of these tools that should definitely be remembered are the principles of generic good practice (GxP) (including Good Laboratory, Good Clinical, Good Manufacturing, Good Distribution and Good Pharmacovigilance Practices), which specify rules and guidelines designed to ensure that all aspects of the pharmaceuticals' development process are conducted following the best methods for quality, safety and efficacy.

Moreover, in order to improve medicines' early access, especially for patients who have a specific condition not adequately addressed by an existing therapy, the so-called adaptive pathways approach was introduced. It is based on existing regulatory procedures, and envisages, though only after initial clinical studies, an advanced approval of a medicine for a restricted number of patients, to progressively expand, thanks to the collected data, that medicine's access to a broader population[151].

All these measures, necessary to deal with the above-mentioned pharmaceutical policies, have been introduced, renewed, and controlled by a precise and *ad hoc* created system of medicine regulation.

---

[149] Pilgerstorfer, "EU Law", 156.

[150] Elias Mossialos, Monique Mrazek and Tom Walley, *Regulating pharmaceuticals in Europe: striving for efficiency, equity and quality* (Maidenhead: Open University Press, 2004), 8.

[151] Nicole Scholz, *Medicinal products in the European Union: The legal framework for medicines for human use* (European Parliamentary Research Service, 2015), 1.

The system is a unique network composed of the 31 European Economic Area[152] (EEA) national competent authorities, the EMA and the Commission, which meets four times a year in a voluntary (non-statutory) forum to discuss issues of strategic importance.

The carrier of the system is represented by a pool of thousands of experts in different sectors who, through the exchange of information, knowledge and best practices, try to achieve the highest standards for medicines' regulation, avoid the duplication of efforts and ensure that patients and healthcare professionals are provided with adequate and consistent information about medicines. The European experts, nominated by the Member States or the EMA, serve as members of the Agency's scientific committees[153] and can only be involved once their declaration of interests has been evaluated.

The network also works thanks to Information Technology (IT) systems, which facilitate the exchange of important information, the supervision of clinical trials and compliance with the different GxP, but especially because European Union legislation requires that each Member State operates according to the same rules and requirements regarding the medicines' authorisation and monitoring.

The European institution that plays an essential role in this regulatory system is the European Medicines Agency (EMA); a decentralised EU agency founded in 1995 as the European Medicines Evaluation Agency (EMEA), currently located in London (but due to move to Amsterdam), and operating on the basis of Regulation (EC) No. 726/2004. Its general role is to protect human and animal health by ensuring medicines' safety, quality and efficacy; a goal achieved through the evaluation of pharmaceuticals' marketing authorisations, the facilitation of medicines' development and access, the control of medicinal products' safety across their life cycle and, lastly, the supply of the relevant information to healthcare professionals and patients.

In doing so, the Agency is provided with a series of updated regulatory mechanisms and a huge number of scientific experts who take part in the EMA's assessment teams, working parties and advisory groups or

---

[152] The European Economic Area united the EU Member States and three other States (Iceland, Liechtenstein, and Norway) into an internal market governed by the same basic rules.

[153] A public list of the names and details of such experts is maintained by the EMA and is available on its website at http://www.ema.europa.eu/ema/index.jsp?curl=pages/about_us/landing/experts.jsp&mid=WC0b01ac058043244a (accessed November 25, 2018).

participate in the seven scientific committees operating for the Agency. Among the experts' many competencies, a prominent role is occupied by the scientific advice, guidelines and support provided to companies developing new medicines, especially in relation to the preparation of the marketing authorisation applications.

The EMA monitors and supervises the safety of medicines continuously, ensuring that their benefits outweigh their risks, especially through the monitoring of companies' compliance with their pharmacovigilance obligations and further contributing to international pharmacovigilance activities with authorities outside the EU. To carry out the coordination of these countries' obligations on pharmacovigilance, for instance, the EMA manages EudraVigilance, the internet-based information system through which patients and health professionals report suspected adverse reactions of any used pharmaceuticals.

Despite the many tasks that the EMA carries out, it must be pointed out that a number of key activities related to this regulatory system for medicines are not the Agency's responsibility. Indeed, *inter alia*, it does not have the legislative power to create laws concerning medicines, it does not take decisions on pharmaceuticals' pricing and reimbursement, it does not carry out research or develop new medicinal products, it does not issue marketing authorisations, it cannot provide medical advice, and it does not deal with medical devices, food supplements or cosmetics.

The EMA charges the holders of marketing authorisations fees for the services it provides, such as the applications or variations of an authorisation and pharmacovigilance activities [154], according to the provisions laid down in the fee Regulation[155] and the pharmacovigilance fee Regulation[156].

---

154 "Fees payable to the European Medicines Agency", European Medicines Agency, accessed November 25, 2018, http://www.ema.europa.eu/ema/index.jsp?curl=pages/regulation/document_listing/document_listing_000327.jsp&mid=WC0b01ac05800245966.

155 Council Regulation (EC) No. 297/95 of 10 February 1995 on fees payable to the European Agency for the Evaluation of Medicinal Products; 1995 O.J. (L 35) 1, http://data.europa.eu/eli/reg/1995/297/2018-04-01.

156 Regulation (EU) No. 658/2014 of the European Parliament and of the Council of 15 May 2014 on fees payable to the European Medicines Agency for the conduct of pharmacovigilance activities in respect of medicinal products for human use; 2014 O.J. (L 189) 112, http://data.europa.eu/eli/reg/2014/658/2018-02-12.

This entire regulatory landscape supervises the safety of medicines during their clinical trials, marketing authorisation, manufacturing, packaging, distribution, retailing, advertising, and pharmacovigilance; each of these will now be treated individually to understand how they operate in the current regulatory system of medicinal products.

1.3.a Clinical Trials

The intricate regulatory system of pharmaceuticals was designed to balance the protection of future patients from harmful medicinal products with, at the same time, the need to develop the beneficial ones[157]. This difficult attempt is handled by European law, which regulates the clinical trials process, by restricting the marketing of risky products and providing compensation for harms caused by them[158].

Let us now deal with the regulation of clinical trials. But first, what is a clinical trial and what is it for? The simplest[159] and most authoritative definition, suitable for a general explanation, is provided by the World Health Organisation (WHO), which advises:

> *(...) a clinical trial is any research study that prospectively assigns human participants or groups of humans to one or more health-related interventions to evaluate the effects on health outcomes[160].*

We are therefore in the first step of medicine safety monitoring.

Once the pharmaceutical, after having been studied and developed in the laboratory, has passed the stage of pre-clinical trials conducted on animals and has proven to be safe and effective, it passes to the clinical phase on human beings. Clinical trials on medicines, before being conducted, have to obtain authorisation from an appropriate national competent authority and approval from a specific ethics committee, which also provides guarantees for the medical staff that will carry out the study.

In the clinical phase, researchers and medicine developers determine the correct dosage and the most appropriate method of administering a new drug, and, most importantly, confirm or disclaim its safety and

---

[157] Hervey and McHale, *European Union Health Law*, 293.

[158] Ibid., 295.

[159] See in this regard the definition of clinical trials provided by Article 1(2), Regulation (EU) No. 536/2014.

[160] "Clinical trials", World Health Organisation, accessed November 25, 2018, http://www.who.int/topics/clinical_trials/en/.

efficacy on human beings by detecting any side effects. Prior to any such study, however, the so-called principal investigator prepares an action plan, describing the goals and methods in which a specific clinical trial will be conducted.

The process of the clinical investigation is normally conducted through three steps, which are necessary to obtain the marketing authorisation for the medicine's use by the general population. Phase I consists of the drug being tested on healthy volunteers and has the aim of determining molecular safety and researching how it works and reacts in the human body. Phase II, testing the product on patients with specific diseases, seeks to assess the efficacy and continues the safety evaluation by especially investigating the possible side effects and risks. Phase III, always conducted on patients, confirms the results and establishes the pharmaceutical therapeutic effect, evaluating, in particular, the benefit-risk, the right patients and the best way to manage the risks. After getting the marketing authorisation, the medicinal products pass to phase IV, which consists of "post-approval" studies and post-marketing surveillance of the drug's long-term effects.

This entire process lasts for many years and requires substantial monetary costs that are generally borne by the drug owner, almost always a pharmaceutical industry.

The European legislation that regulates the entire above-described process is the Clinical Trials Directive, which has been steadily replaced by the Clinical Trials Regulation.

The first historical reason that led the legislator to deal with this matter can be found in the need to give an ethical framework to all the clinical research, with a particular focus on the protection of human rights. In addition, three other rationales apply: the patient safety ensured by the mandatory compliance with "good clinical practice"; the public safety and interest guaranteed by inspections and surveillance; and the efficient development of scientific research, facilitated by speeding up the approval procedure of the trials. Indeed, if the trials are unsafe and cause harm to patients, considerable reputational damages can occur, leading to a consequent adverse financial impact upon the research organisation and the pharmaceutical industry. It requires a continuous balance between the different rationales, which are also, on the other hand, mutually supportive[161].

[161] Hervey and McHale, *European Union Health Law*, 302-303.

The Clinical Trials Directive was adopted especially in order to facilitate consistency in the pharmaceutical approval processes, but because of the different interpretations and approaches taken by Member States in the implementation of the Directive's ethical underpinnings, this goal has never been achieved. The Clinical Trials Regulation is a response to this failure. First of all, being a Regulation, it is directly applicable in the national legal frameworks, reducing Member States' power of discretion; secondly, and more importantly, it recognises the variety of the national approaches adopted in the trial's approval, especially in relation to ethical concerns.

Although the Regulation entered into force in 2014, the timing of its application will be confirmed by an independent audit, after which the EU clinical trials portal and database will be effectively functional.

The Regulation expands the scope of the Directive and focuses on the multi-centred trials across Member States and how the latter have to cooperate in the authorisation process.

In order to be assessed, the application of any clinical trials conducted in the Union must first be registered in an *ad hoc* created single EU entry point (the EU portal) to submit the relative required information to be stored in a database (the EU database)[162], facilitating in this way the application for clinical trials' authorisation as well as the access to clinical trials' information and assessments carried out by Member States.

Moreover, the Regulation creates a single authorisation procedure for all the trials, ensuring, in this way, greater consistency and one single assessment outcome per Member State. To further speed up the procedure, if the competent national authority fails to report within the deadline, tacit approval will be assumed, thus giving sponsors and researchers more legal certainty.

Furthermore, the concept of "reporting" Member States is introduced. This means that the applicant, in order to obtain an authorisation, will submit, thought the EU portal, a dossier to the Member States concerned, proposing one of them as the reporting one which, for its part, can accept or refuse it within six days[163]. In other words, an applicant will propose a specific Member State that will be able to respond more promptly and with a higher level of scientific rigor to the ethical and scientific aspects of the clinical study than the other countries of the European Union.

The assigned reporting Member State will complete "Part I" of the assessment report dealing with the specific matters listed in Article 6 of

---

[162] Regulation (EU) No. 536/2014, Articles 80 and 81.

[163] Ibid., Article 5.

the Regulation, such as, *inter alia*, compliance with the requirements concerning the manufacturing and import of investigational pharmaceuticals; the completeness and adequateness of the investigator's brochure; and compliance with the labelling requirements. Things get complicated in relation to the aspects covered in "Part II"[164] of the assessment report. Indeed, all Member States concerned shall assess, each for their own territory, various ethical and human rights aspects, leaving, in this way, considerable scope for the adoption of different approaches among the Member States, thus further slowing down the desired process towards harmonisation[165].

On the other hand, sponsorship is facilitated by the Regulation, providing that a trial may have several sponsors all subjected to the obligations of sponsorship unless otherwise determined in a specific contract[166].

The Regulation also deals with the protection of rights, dignity, well-being and other ethical aspects. In this respect, it is important to note the new provisions on informed consent, which, in line with the recent update of the Declaration of Helsinki[167], can be obtained after the decision is made to include the patient in the clinical trial if the specific conditions listed in Article 35, such as the urgency of the situation, are fulfilled.

Furthermore, the Regulation finally establishes reasonable and clear rules to facilitate the inclusion of the critical patient in dedicated trials. The new legislation provides that, under emergency conditions, in the face of a rigorous protocol of study and approval by an ethics committee, the expert clinician is in a better position than a family member to evaluate the critical patient's involvement in a dedicated clinical trial[168].

The Regulation has also strengthened the transparency of clinical data, stating that the sponsor has to report the trial's start and end to the Member States. Moreover, when the clinical trial is to be used to support a future marketing authorisation, a clinical study report, as defined in Article 2(25), must be submitted to the EU database. However, for unsuccessful trials, the sponsor is under an obligation to submit a summary of their results after one year. Another relevant problem is that the Regulation only

---

[164] Ibid., Article 7.

[165] Hervey and McHale, *European Union Health Law*, 308.

[166] Regulation (EU) No. 536/2014, Article 72.

[167] World Medical Association, *Declaration of Helsinki.*

[168] Stefano Savonitto et al., "Il consenso informato alla sperimentazione clinica nel paziente critico. Introduzione al Regolamento UE n. 536/2014 sulla sperimentazione clinica di medicinali per uso umano che abroga la Direttiva 2001/20/EC", *Giornale Italiano di Cardiologia* 17, no. 5 (May 2016): 326-334.

applies to new medicinal products, thus leaving unresolved the problem of the data's lack of transparency on existing medicines and studies conducted before the entry into force of this law[169].

Additionally, according to Articles 56 and 57, data must be collected and stored with the aim of ensuring the safety of patients and effective monitoring and reporting, proving the focus on scientific risk assessment within the Regulation[170].

Finally, another important aspect to be reported in this brief summary on the innovations introduced by the Regulation is the simplification of the rules on safety reporting. First of all, the European Medicines Agency has been invested with the task of organizing and maintaining the EudraVigilance database[171], an electronic database for the reporting, by the sponsor, of Suspected Unexpected Serious Adverse Reactions (SUSARs)[172] as well as an annual report on investigational medicinal products (other than placebos) on the safety of each investigational medicinal product used in a clinical trial for which it is the sponsor[173].

The simplification consists of the fact that, first, in the case of a clinical trial involving the use of more than one investigational medicinal product, the sponsor may submit a single safety report on all investigational medicinal products used in that clinical trial[174]; second, that the protocol may provide that not all adverse events and serious adverse events are recorded and reported; and third, the use of the EudraVigilance database for the reports of the SUSARs.

Numerous criticisms and concerns have been raised about the new provisions. The European Group on Ethics in Science and New Technologies (EGE) has expressed doubts about the administrative complexity and the onerousness of the documentation relating to the clinical trial to be submitted by the applicant in the submission for its authorisation[175].

---

169 Hervey and McHale, *European Union Health Law*, 320.
170 Ibid., 310.
171 Regulation (EU) No. 536/2014, Article 40.
172 Ibid., Article 42.
173 Ibid., Article 43.
174 Ibid., Article 43(2).
175 European Group on Ethics in Science and New Technologies, *Statement of the European Group on Ethics in Science and New Technologies on the Proposal for a Regulation of the European Parliament and the Council on Clinical Trials on Medicinal Products for Human Use and repealing Directive 2001/20/EC*, COM (2012) 369 final, 4, para 10.

Furthermore, the Regulation, according to Article 4, requires that the timelines for ethical review must be compatible with the timelines and procedures for the trial's authorisation, thus reducing the protection of patients. Moreover, the Regulation leaves considerable differences existing between Member States, in particular regarding ethical and human rights aspects[176].

A further criticism was made about the fact that full data-sharing of the mandatory clinical trial master file, as stated in Article 36, is on a voluntary basis only, thus reducing attempts to impose greater transparency.

Finally, concerns remain about the functioning of the new EU portal and database and how they will interact with the already existing EU clinical trials database system, the EudraCT system[177].

All we have to do is wait for the Regulation to enter into application, currently estimated to occur in 2019, to see if the desired objectives, in particular those of the simplification and harmonisation of the administrative provisions governing clinical trials in the Union, will be achieved.

1.3.b Marketing Authorisation

After the clinical trials, in order to protect public health and ensure that the criteria of pharmaceuticals' quality, safety and efficacy are fulfilled, all medicinal products have to be authorised either at Member State or Community level before they can be placed on the EU market.

It is important to remember that the marketing authorisations cannot be released if the principles of good laboratory and clinical practice are not respected[178].

The European regulatory system for medicines provides two different routes for marketing authorisation and only one set of common EU rules. Indeed, despite the various authorisation procedures, the rules and requirements applicable to pharmaceuticals in the EU are the same.

First, the authorisation can be released by the national competent authority of a Member State in accordance with Directive 2001/83/EC, following, as appropriate, the individual Member State's application, the decentralised procedure or mutual recognition.

Second, in some specific cases and following the procedure established in Regulation (EC) No. 726/2004, the applicant can apply to the EMA via

---

[176] Hervey and McHale, *European Union Health Law*, 308.

[177] The EudraCT system is available online at https://eudract.ema.europa.eu/ (accessed November 27, 2018).

[178] Hervey and McHale, *European Union Health Law*, 327.

the centralised procedure and, after the Agency has made the relative assessment, the Commission decides whether to grant the marketing authorisation, which is valid across the Union as well as in the European Economic Area.

The centralised procedure is compulsory for producers of medicinal products listed in the Annex of Regulation (EC) No. 726/2004: products developed by means of some specific biotechnological process; orphan and advanced therapy medicines; medicinal products for veterinary use intended primarily as performance enhancers in order to promote the growth of treated animals or to increase yields from treated animals; and medicinal products for human use containing a new active substance for which the therapeutic indication is the treatment of AIDS, cancer, neurodegenerative disorders, diabetes, and auto-immune and viral diseases. Instead, this procedure is optional if medicines contain a new active substance which was not authorised in the EU as of 20 May 2004; or if the product constitutes a significant therapeutic, scientific or technical innovation[179]; or if it is in the interests of public or animal health at Union level. In these cases, the manufacturers cannot make current applications under both the Regulation and the Directive[180].

In all other circumstances and for all other medicinal products not mentioned above, the applicant must apply to a national competent authority via the decentralised or mutual recognition procedures if s/he wants to authorise a medicine in several Member States.

There are also additional authorisation procedures for some specific types of medicines (orphan, geriatric, paediatric, herbal, homeopathic, advanced-therapy and non-prescription medicines), each one of which has its own particular regulation[181].

Individual Member State Application

In order to obtain an authorisation to place a medicinal product in only one EU country's market, a specific application shall be submitted to the national competent authority of the Member State concerned. According to Article 8 of the Community Code Directive, the application shall be accompanied by particulars and documents, such as, for instance, the

---

179 Regulation (EC) No. 726/2004, Article 3(2) and Article 90.

180 European Commission, *Commission communication on the Community marketing authorisation procedures for medicinal products*, 1988 O.J. (C 229) 4. Where there are different therapeutic indications, there is a possible exception to this principle.

181 Pilgerstorfer, "EU Law", 161.

description of the manufacturing method, the therapeutic indications, contra-indications and adverse reactions, the results of all trial stages and the description of the control methods employed by the manufacturer. Moreover, the applicant must include the document describing the Summary of Product Characteristics (SPC), the mock-ups of the outer packaging and a draft package leaflet. In 2010, in response to the numerous critics of the pharmaceutical industry's lack of transparency over previous marketing authorisation refusals, additional information to be included in the application, namely

> *(...) details of any decision to refuse authorisation, whether in the Union or in a third country, and the reasons for such a decision*[182],

was introduced[183].

Articles 10-10c of the Directive specify a series of derogations from the obligation to provide the results of pharmaceutical (physico-chemical, biological or microbiological) and pre-clinical (toxicological and pharmacological) tests, and clinical trials[184] for, *inter alia*, generics, biosimilar products, or medicinal products, in which the active substances have been in well-established medicinal use for at least ten years. It is also underlined that these derogations should not prejudice the law relating to the protection of industrial and commercial property.

After the submission of the application, the national competent authority concerned examines if the conditions for granting the marketing authorisation have been fulfilled[185]. In order to make such an assessment, the authority may: require further information from the applicant[186]; check whether the manufacturer can produce the product in compliance with the referred details[187]; or submit the medicinal product for testing by an official laboratory in order to ensure that the control methods employed by the manufacturer are satisfactory[188].

According to Article 17(1), Member States shall take all appropriate measures to ensure that the entire procedure is completed within a maximum of 210 days.

---

182 Directive 2001/83/EC, Article 8(3)(1).
183 Hervey and McHale, *European Union Health Law*, 331.
184 Directive 2001/83/EC, Article 8(3)(j).
185 Ibid., Article 19(1).
186 Ibid., Article 19(3).
187 Ibid., Article 20(a).
188 Ibid., Article 19(2).

Where the competent authority decides to grant the marketing authorisation because the criteria laid down in Article 26 for the refusal of the application have not been fulfilled, further conditions with deadlines may be imposed on the producer (for example, the obligation to conduct a post-authorisation safety study or a post-authorisation efficacy study)[189]. Finally, in the event that an authorisation is granted and, according to Article 21, the national competent authority has to approve the SPC and formulate a report explaining their assessment, then, without delay, the authority has to make publicly available the marketing authorisation, the package leaflet, the SPC, and the specific additional conditions for each authorised medicine.

A marketing authorisation, granted following both the individual Member State's application and the decentralised procedure, is valid for five years and may be renewed after five years on the basis of a re-evaluation of the risk-benefit balance by the competent authority of the authorising Member State[190]. Once renewed, the marketing authorisation shall be valid for an unlimited period unless the authority decides, on justified grounds relating to pharmacovigilance, to proceed with one additional five-year renewal. Moreover, according to Article 24, the authorisation ceases to be valid if the authorised medicine is not placed on the market within three years of its granting or if, once placed on the market, it is not sold for three consecutive years.

Finally, the authorisation may be refused or revoked by the competent authority if the risk-benefit balance is not or is no longer considered to be favourable; if the therapeutic efficacy is insufficient; if the qualitative and quantitative composition is not as declared; or if the marketing authorisation holder did not fulfil specific legal obligations[191]. In case of authorisation refusal, the authority must in any case justify such a decision and notify the applicant, who, in turn, may lodge an objection to the refusal under the provisions set out by national law.

Decentralised Procedure and Mutual Recognition

The majority of medicines must be authorised by competent national authorities following the procedure laid down in Article 28 of Directive 2001/83/EC, which in the first paragraph states:

---

[189] Ibid., Article 22a.

[190] Ibid., Article 24.

[191] Ibid., Article 26.

With a view to the granting of a marketing authorisation for a medicinal product in more than one Member State, an applicant shall submit an application based on an identical dossier in these Member States.

Therefore, when an applicant wants to obtain a marketing authorisation in more than one Member State, he can use the mutual recognition procedure if the manufacturer has already obtained authorisation in one Member State, or the decentralised procedure if the medicine has not yet been authorised in any EU country and does not fall within the compulsory scope of the centralised procedure.

Under the decentralised procedure, which is the successor of the "multi-state procedure", the manufacturer simultaneously submits the applications based on an identical dossier to all national competent authorities concerned, asking only one of them to be the reference one. The reference Member State has to conduct a fresh assessment within 120 days and send the report to the other national authorities involved and, like in the mutual recognition procedure, the decision of this competent authority must be recognised by the other Member States concerned, following the same approval procedure provided for by the mutual recognition procedure.

Indeed, the mutual recognition procedure is very similar to the decentralised one, but because the assessment by the competent authority is based on an already authorised medicine, it must be completed within fewer days (90 instead of 120). The producer sends the application based on an identical dossier, containing the information and documents described above in the individual application, to each Member State in which he seeks recognition and names the Reference Member State (RMS) which has already authorised the product involved. The RMS also has to prepare an updated assessment report within 90 days and then transmit it, together with the SPC, labelling and package leaflet, to all the Member States concerned for approval, to be released within another 90 days[192].

For both procedures and according to Article 29, when there is a "*potential serious risk to public health*" a Member State can deny the request for approval, giving a detailed exposition of its reasons. Such points of disagreement shall be forthwith referred to the Coordination Group for Mutual Recognition and Decentralised Procedures – Human (CMDh)[193], which considers the matter and strives to reach an agreement within 60 days. If this is not possible, the Member State responsible for the product brings the case to the Committee for Medicinal Products for

---

[192] Pilgerstorfer, "EU Law", 163.

[193] Directive 2001/83/EC, Article 29(1).

Human Use's (CHMP) attention for arbitration. Any failure to agree must be decided by a binding decision of the Commission. After all the Member States involved have approved the documents, each one of them must decide about the authorisation in conformity with the approved assessment report, SPC, labelling and package leaflet within 30 days[194].

Despite the prospect of common regulatory outcomes across the EU and the indisputable saving of energy and costs supported by applicants for obtaining authorisation in multiple jurisdictions, serious concerns about both procedures have been raised. The fact that the system leaves the decision concerning which Member State will be the reference one to the applicants provokes a "race to the bottom" in terms of security standards, which goes against the primary purpose of the entire regulatory system, namely the protection of human health[195]. Indeed, the system incentivises pharmaceutical industries to choose the regulatory agency with the quickest, most cost-effective and least demanding approach to regulation[196].

However, there is a safeguard for Member States who want to oppose the reference Member State's assessment, which is first to address the EMA and, ultimately, the Commission in order to resolve the issue of the standard that should be adopted across the EU[197].

Centralised Procedure

As already explained above, the centralised procedure allows the marketing of a specific medicinal product on the basis of a single EU-wide assessment aimed at obtaining a single marketing authorisation valid across the Union and with the same status of the authorisation granted by the national competent authorities in accordance with the other procedures[198]. Following the provisions laid down in Regulation (EC) No. 726/2004, pharmaceutical companies submit a single application to the EMA containing similar information to that required by the Community Code Directive, with additional requirements in case of the presence of genetically modified organisms[199]. The Agency's CHMP has to carry out

---

[194] Ibid., Article 28(5).
[195] Hervey and McHale, *European Union Health Law*, Chapter 2.
[196] Pilgerstorfer, "EU Law", 164.
[197] Ibid., 165.
[198] Regulation (EC) No. 726/2004, Article 13(1).
[199] Ibid., Article 6(2).

the scientific assessment of the application within 210 days [200] in accordance with the same provisions laid down in the Community Code Directive in relation to the assessment by the competent authorities. Subsequently, the CHMP gives a recommendation to the European Commission on whether or not to grant the relative marketing authorisation. Where the opinion of the Committee is that the application should be refused (on the same basis established by the Directive), some conditions should be imposed on the authorisation, or the SPC need to be amended, or the applicant may give written notice to the Agency specifying that he wishes to request a re-examination of the opinion. Within 60 days the CHMP shall re-examine its opinion, annexing the reasons for its conclusion[201].

Within 15 days of the receipt of the Committee's opinion, the Commission formulates a draft decision, which also has to be forwarded to Member States and the applicant who may participate in its scrutiny in a procedure before the CHMP[202]. At the end,

> *(...) the Commission shall take a final decision in accordance with, and within 15 days after the end of, the procedure (...)*[203].

There are different types of marketing authorisation that can be granted following the centralised procedure. The ordinary one has an initial period duration of five years, which can be re-evaluated by the EMA for an unlimited period[204]. Otherwise it may be that the Commission, on justified grounds relating to pharmacovigilance, proceeds with one additional five-year renewal[205]. Article 14(7) provides a further alternative: a conditional authorisation imposing obligations on the holder, valid for a one-year period and reviewable annually.

In order to increase transparency and in response to some criticism, the Community Register of Medicinal Products has been made available[206], a

[200] According to Article 6(3) of the Regulation, the period may be extended if a reasoned request is promulgated, or, according to Article 14(9), alternatively abridged to 150 days where the product is of major interest from the point of view of public health and therapeutic innovation.

[201] Regulation (EC) No. 726/2004, Article 9(1).

[202] Ibid., Articles 10 and 87.

[203] Ibid., Article 10(2).

[204] Ibid., Article 14(1).

[205] Ibid., Article 14(3).

[206] The Community Register of Medicinal Products is available online at http://ec.europa.eu/health/documents/community-register/html/index_en.htm (accessed November 27, 2018).

public list containing all the medicinal products which obtained their marketing authorisation in accordance with the centralised procedure.

The introduction of the centralised procedure was welcomed especially by European pharmaceutical companies operating in the global market, in particular for its significant efficiency gains and the quicker returns on investment in developing novel medicinal products[207].

Moreover, this system, being fully harmonised across Member States, does not cause the same race to the bottom as happens with the mutual recognition and the decentralised procedures.

Generally speaking, in addition to the possible obligations and conditions imposed on the producer for a particular type of marketing authorisation, both the Directive and the Regulation impose additional duties on the authorisation holder[208]: scientific and technical progress must be taken into account; required and approved changes must be introduced by the holder in order to enable the medicinal product to be manufactured and checked by generally accepted scientific methods; and amendments to the information or documents provided in the dossier must be provided to the regulator[209]. Moreover, other specific duties are imposed on the authorisation holder during the process of pharmacovigilance.

Notwithstanding these duties, after the marketing authorisation has been granted, the producer can shift its focus from research and development to marketing[210].

1.3.c Manufacturing

Prior to the commencement of production, in order to mass produce medicines, pharmaceutical manufacturers must obtain a manufacturing authorisation, which consequently triggers an inspection of their Good Manufacturing Practices (GMP).

The GMP is a set of quality standards ensuring that a medicinal product fulfils the minimum requirements set by specific guidelines that a manufacturer must meet in order to ensure that the medicine is safe, of a high quality and effective.

---

[207] Hervey and McHale, *European Union Health Law*, 329.

[208] See Directive 2001/83/EC, Article 23 and Regulation (EC) No. 726/2004, Article 16.

[209] Pilgerstorfer, “EU Law”, 170.

[210] Emily Jackson, *Law and Regulation of Medicines* (Oxford: Hart Publishing, 2012), 73.

In accordance with Article 47 of Directive 2001/83/EC, the Commission has adopted the principles and guidelines of the GMP for medicinal products in the form of Commission Directive 2003/94/EC[211] concerning medicinal products for human use and investigational medicinal products, with the further aim of ensuring the harmonised application of these requirements across the Union[212]. In addition, the Commission has published detailed GMP guidelines in line with those principles, in collaboration with the EMA, in EudraLex-Volume 4[213], which are revised on a regular basis.

The manufacturing authorisation is granted by national competent authorities and entered into the EudraGMDP, a publicly available European database operated by the EMA containing information about the manufacturing and import authorisations, GMP certificates, statements of non-compliance with GMP and GMP inspection planning in third countries.

Member States are under the obligation to take all appropriate measures to ensure that the manufacture of the medicinal products within their territory is subject to the holding of a manufacturing authorisation[214]. It is important to underline that the marketing authorisation holder and the manufacturer authorisation holder are not always the same person[215], thus the two positions entail different obligations.

According to Article 46(f) of the Community Code Directive:

> *(...) the holder of a manufacturing authorisation shall at least be obliged to comply with the principles and guidelines of good manufacturing practice for medicinal products and to use only active substances, which have been manufactured in accordance with good manufacturing practice for active substances and distributed in accordance with good distribution practices for active substances.*

It is also important to underline that the GMP guidelines are not prescriptive instructions on how to manufacture medicinal products, but only a series of general principles that must be observed during manufacturing and that comprise criteria referring to quality management,

---

211 Commission Directive 2003/94/EC of 8 October 2003 lays down the principles and guidelines of good manufacturing practice in respect of medicinal products for human use and investigational medicinal products for human use; 2003 O.J. (L 262) 22, http://data.europa.eu/eli/dir/2003/94/oj.

212 Scholz, *Medicinal Products,* 20.

213 European Commission, "EudraLex-Volume 4"

214 Directive 2001/83/EC, Article 40(1).

215 European Commission, "EudraLex-Volume 4", Chapter 7, para 7.3.

personnel, premises and equipment, documentation, production, quality control, contracting out and self-inspection[216].

A pharmaceutical company, in setting up its manufacturing program, can decide the most effective and efficient quality process to fulfil its GMP requirements. It is also important to note that if producers choose to follow other processes, then they will have to prove their conformity by showing the equivalence of those standards to those set out in Directive 2003/94/EC. In fact, the responsibility to ensure and certify that the medicinal products are produced in compliance with the GMP and in accordance with the marketing authorisations belongs to a specific qualified person[217]. If the holder of the marketing authorisation himself fulfils the conditions of qualification set out in Article 49 of the Community Code Directive, then he may himself assume such a responsibility[218].

According to the GMP guidelines, manufacturing facilities must be clean, hygienic and organised in adequate premises and spaces; environmental conditions need to be controlled in order to prevent cross contamination; and the producer must work with suitable equipment, services, storage, transport, containers and labels. The manufacturer should have an adequate number of appropriately qualified and trained personnel with the necessary qualifications and practical experience. Moreover, every person entering the manufacturing areas should wear protective garments appropriate to the operations to be carried out. Generally speaking, all the manufacturing processes must be checked and documented in such a way as to track the complete history of a batch, allowing for its possible withdrawal from the market in case of future problems.

Finally, Article 46b of the Community Code Directive states that all these provisions also apply to medicines intended for export, as well as to medicines and active substances imported into the EU. Indeed, active substances must be accompanied by a written confirmation from the competent authority of the exporting third country that the GMP standards in the manufacturing site are equivalent to those of the EU.

---

216 Scholz, *Medicinal Products,* 20.

217 A person that fulfils the conditions of qualification set out in paras 2 and 3 of Article 49 of Directive 2001/83/EC.

218 Directive 2001/83/EC, Article 48(2).

1.3.d Packaging and Labelling

After manufacturing, the medicinal product, before being distributed to retailers and pharmacies throughout the EU, must be properly packaged. The Community Code Directive describes the various particulars that must be included in the labelling, packaging and leaflets of each medicine.

There is a list detailing the compulsory packaging information that must be clearly reported in each pack, such as the name of the medicinal product, its strength, the total content of the package, how to administer it, the expiry date, the target group it is intended for, any special warnings, instructions for use (for non-prescription medicines), the marketing authorisation number and the name and address of the authorisation holder[219]. The information presented on/within the package must be clear, legible, useful and easily understandable; for this reason, particulars are to be written in the official language of the Member State where the product is placed on the market[220]. It has been pointed out that this latter requirement is a serious impediment to the creation of a true single market of pharmaceuticals but, given that there are no legal impediments, it is simply a matter of logistics since the physical space on the packaging is not sufficient for the translation of the compulsory information into several languages[221]. Moreover, when the medicinal products contain certain substances, special warnings and resistant packaging are required in order to prevent their accidental use by children.

The Community Code Directive also regulates the use of package leaflets[222], which must be drawn up to respect the SPC and must include detailed information such as the identification of the product, its therapeutic indications, contra-indications, precautions for use, interactions with other medical products, special warnings, instructions for use, adverse reactions, expiry date, the name and address of the manufacturer and marketing authorisation holder, and the date on which the package leaflet was last updated.

The European legislator has introduced special labelling for medicinal products that are monitored very closely by regulatory authorities – not because they are unsafe, as one might immediately think, but due to the little information available about them (for example, because they are new

---

219 Ibid., Articles 54-55.
220 Ibid., Article 63(1).
221 Hervey and McHale, *European Union Health Law*, 337.
222 Directive 2001/83/EC, Articles 58-60.

to the market). Medicinal products "under additional monitoring" have a black inverted triangle displayed on their package leaflet[223].

Figure 1-2 The black triangle on the leaflets of medicines under additional monitoring[224]

The reason behind all these information requirements is consumer protection. In this way, appropriately informed patients are able to determine whether the risks associated with the use of the medicines are acceptable to them.

EU packaging and labelling rules imply, in this way, an approach to risk that leaves significant responsibilities to the consumers, especially in taking the relevant described precautions. This more subjective approach has been adopted by the European legislator in an age of wide access to information through the Internet and the increasing number of online pharmacies, a fact that increase the consumers' awareness[225].

1.3.e Distribution

Once properly packaged, medicinal products are ready for distribution: an increasingly complex system involving many players and consisting of several stages such as handling, transportation and storage.

---

[223] Commission implementing Regulation (EU) No. 198/2013 of 7 March 2013 on the selection of a symbol for the purpose of identifying medicinal products for human use that are subject to additional monitoring; 2013 O.J. (L 65) 17, http://data.europa.eu/eli/reg_impl/2013/198/oj.

[224] Data source: "What does the black triangle mean?", European Medicines Agency, accessed November 28, 2018, https://www.ema.europa.eu/documents/other/what-does-black-triangle-mean_en.pdf.

[225] Hervey and McHale, *European Union Health Law*, 338-339.

In order to support wholesale distributors in their duties, but also with the further aims of preventing falsified medicines from entering the legal supply chain and maintaining the quality and integrity of products, the European Commission has published, since 1994, EU Guidelines on Good Distribution Practice (GDP).

The present guidelines[226], revised in 2013 in order to consider the advances in practices for the appropriate distribution of medicines, as well as new requirements introduced by Directive 2011/62/EU, are based on Articles 84 and 85b(3) of the Community Code Directive.

According to Article 1(17) of Directive 2001/83/EC, the wholesale distribution of medicinal products comprises:

> *(...) all activities consisting of procuring, holding, supplying or exporting medicinal products, apart from supplying medicinal products to the public. Such activities are carried out with manufacturers or their depositories, importers, other wholesale distributors or with pharmacists and persons authorised or entitled to supply medicinal products to the public in the Member State concerned.*

Any person acting as a wholesale distributor has to hold a wholesale distribution authorisation and must comply with the principles of guidelines for GDP[227].

Such guidelines cover many aspects of the distribution chain: the management system; the responsible personnel, who must undergo specific training; special requirements for the protection of hygiene, the premises and equipment, especially in relation to temperature and environmental control; compulsory documentation; the rules about storage, supply, transportation and export to third countries; and self-inspections, suspected medicinal products and complaints.

Generally speaking, the person responsible for the distribution must follow detailed procedures in order to protect pharmaceuticals against breakage, contamination and theft as well as from the harmful effects of light, temperature, moisture and other external factors. By way of example, and among other duties, medicinal products should be handled and stored in such a way as to prevent spillage, adulteration and mix-ups; distributors should ensure that all vehicles and equipment used are appropriately equipped; a series of procedures for investigating and

---

[226] Guidelines of 5 November 2013 on Good Distribution Practice of medicinal products for human use 2013/C 343/01; 2013 O.J. (C 343) 1, https://eur-lex.europa.eu/LexUriServ/LexUriServ.do?uri=OJ:C:2013:343:0001:0014:EN:PDF

[227] Directive 2001/83/EC, Article 80(g).

handling damages should be set out; all personnel involved in wholesale distribution activities should be trained in the requirements of the GDP prior to commencing their tasks; and a self-inspection program should be implemented covering all aspects of compliance with the GDP and its regulations.

Once the product has safely arrived at the licensed retailer or pharmacy and has been safely stored according to the GDP, the product is ready to be sold to the general public.

1.3.f Retailers

The regulation of pharmaceutical retailers remains the competence of the Member States. The relevant national legislations cover all aspects of the pharmaceutical resale system: from the control of the pharmaceutical job sector to establishment criteria including licensing and geographical restrictions; from the pharmacies' profit and prices to restrictions on the pharmacies' ownership; from the mandatory product range to competition law.[228]

The lack of European harmonisation on these issues entails a wide variety of regulatory approaches and a strong fragmentation of the market structure with important economic and administrative consequences. In this environment, significant differences, propagated by national regulation and historical patterns, exist in terms of remuneration schemes, the operational features of retailers, the number of wholesalers and pharmacies in the Member States, and developments in policy and practice concerning distribution[229].

The attention to the pharmacy sector by European law started in around the mid-2000s, especially in relation to restrictions on the sale of non-prescription-only ("over-the-counter") medicinal products. In this regard, of great significance was the suggestion made by the Estonian Competition Authority in its 2009 Annual Report[230], which called for the opening up of over-the-counter pharmaceuticals sales to the supermarket sector in order to considerably reduce their prices. Indeed, it was

---

228 Hervey and McHale, *European Union Health Law*, 252.

229 Panos Kanavos, Willemien Schurer and Sabine Vogler, "The pharmaceutical distribution chain in the European Union: structure and impact on pharmaceutical prices" (Final Report, European Commission, Brussels, 2011), 12-23, http://eprints.lse.ac.uk/51051/1/Kanavos_pharmaceutical_distribution_chain_2007.pdf.

230 Estonian Competition Authority, 'Annual Report 2009', 2009, 19-21, http://www.konkurentsiamet.ee/public/AnnualReports_/Annual_Report_2009.pdf.

underlined that there was no justification for the anti-competitive policy, which restricted the sale of such products in the name of consumer protection, considering that consumers were purchasing these medicines in pharmacies without consulting pharmacists[231].

Moreover, some EU countries, such as Ireland and the Netherlands, have adopted a less restrictive approach in the regulation of pharmacies based on consumer choice justifications[232].

It is also important to note that this sector has been subject to a series of anti-competitive behaviours and infringement proceedings by the European Commission against several Member States. In particular, in order to verify compliance with EU law, there was scrutiny of, *inter alia*, national collusive arrangements for the sale by pharmacies of prescription medicines; negotiations over medicinal prices; ownership rules and limits on the choice of legal form; discriminatory licensing provisions; and territorial planning legislations about pharmacies[233].

Furthermore, the profession of pharmacists is also highly regulated. Specific legislations of entry, conduct, price, opening hours and training are needed in order to ensure a minimum quality of and adequate access to pharmacists' services. However, such regulations should not restrict competition more than necessary and should be justified and proportional, especially when they serve private interests rather than the public interest[234].

It is definitely worth noting the point of view of the CJEU on the pharmacist's professional figure as not simply being like an economic actor, but also as a public servant, who must maintain, in carrying out his duties, an ethical conduct:

> *It is undeniable that an operator having the status of pharmacist pursues, like other persons, the objective of making a profit. However, as a pharmacist by profession, he is presumed to operate the pharmacy not with a purely economic objective, but also from a professional viewpoint. His private interest connected with the making a profit is thus tempered by his training, by his professional experience and by the responsibility which he owes, given that any breach of the rules of law or professional conduct*

[231] Hervey and McHale, *European Union Health Law*, 252-253.
[232] Ibid., 252.
[233] Ibid., 252-258.
[234] Kanavos, Schurer and Vogler, "Pharmaceutical distribution", 12-23.

undermines not only the value of his investment but also his own professional existence[235].

This view is also recognizable in EU health law.

As has already been seen in the developments of the EU legislation on medicinal products due to the increasing illegal sale of medicines to the public via the Internet by retailers operating outside the law, the EU has introduced new rules with Directive 2011/62/EU in order to curb the phenomenon of the market circulation of falsified medicines. In this regard, it is worth remembering the introduction of a common logo to identify the legally operating online pharmacies/retailers in Member States. Buying medicines from a legally operating pharmacy or retailer guarantees the safety and quality of the products.

1.3.g Advertising

European Union law controls the advertising of medicines and provides for special rules and prohibitions in the Community Code Directive[236].

The Directive defines advertising as

(...) any form of door-to-door information, canvassing activity or inducement designed to promote the prescription, supply, sale or consumption of medicinal products[237].

The above-mentioned definition has been widely interpreted by the CJEU to include third-party activity, such as journalism or the use of the Internet intended to promote products classified as pharmaceuticals[238], with the objective of safeguarding human health. The CJEU has also stated that the advertising rules laid down in the Directive also cover quotations taken from medical journals or other scientific works which are included in advertisements for medicinal products directed to persons qualified to

---

[235] Joined Cases C-171/07 and C-172/07, Apothekerkammer des Saarlandes and Others (C-171/07) and Helga Neumann-Seiwert (C-172/07) v. Saarland and Ministerium für Justiz, Gesundheit und SozialesNeumann-Siewert, 2009 E.C.R. I-04171, EU:C:2009:316, para 37.

[236] Directive 2001/83/EC, Articles 86-100.

[237] Ibid., Article 86.

[238] Case C-421/07, Criminal proceedings v. Frede Damgaard, 2009 E.C.R. I-02629, EU:C:2009:222.

prescribe or supply medicines; their source must be clearly identified in order to let health professionals verify them[239].

Before medicinal products can be advertised, Member States must ensure that they have a marketing authorisation[240], because only authorised over-the-counter pharmaceuticals [241] can be advertised to consumers directly. Indeed, it is specifically stated that Member States shall prohibit the advertising to the general public of medicinal products which are only available on medical prescription or contain substances defined as psychotropic or narcotic by international convention[242]. Moreover, it is left to the discretion of the Member States to ban the advertising of medicines that are reimbursable by their national health insurance system [243]. However, at the same time, given that national schemes that encourage the prescription of cheaper generics are not classified as commercial promotions, they cannot be prohibited[244].

Any advertising to the general public of a medicinal product must comply with the particulars listed in the relevant SPC[245]; must encourage the rational use of the product without exaggeration; and, more importantly, must not be misleading[246]. All advertising must be clearly identifiable; provide the name of the product; instructions on how to use it correctly; and a specific and legible invitation to read all the instructions carefully[247]. It is also provided that the advertising of a medicinal product shall not contain any material which, *inter alia*, gives the impression that a medical consultation or operation is unnecessary; suggests that the use of a medicine is not accompanied by adverse reactions; suggests that the health of the subject can be enhanced by taking the medicine or, on the contrary, could be affected by not taking the medicine[248]; suggests that the safety or efficacy of the medicinal product is due to the fact that it is natural; or

---

239 Case C-249/09, Novo Nordisk AS v. Ravimiamet, 2011 E.C.R. I-03155, ECLI:EU:C:2011:272.

240 Directive 2001/83/EC, Article 87.

241 Ibid., Article 88(1). As stated in Article 88(4), only officially supported vaccination campaigns are exempted.

242 Directive 2001/83/EC, Article 88(1).

243 Ibid., Article 88(3).

244 Case C-62/09, The Queen, on the application of Association of the British Pharmaceutical Industry v. Medicines and Healthcare Products Regulatory Agency, 2010 E.C.R. I-03603, EU:C:2010:219.

245 Directive 2001/83/EC, Article 87(2).

246 Ibid., Article 87(3).

247 Ibid., Article 89(1).

248 This specific prohibition does not apply to vaccination campaigns.

refers, in improper, alarming or misleading terms, to claims of recovery[249]. Furthermore, even the distribution of free samples of medicines is expressly regulated in order to be provided only on an exceptional basis and only to persons qualified to prescribe them in specific conditions[250].

It is naturally left to Member States to organise a national system designed to ensure adequate and effective methods to monitor the advertising of medicinal products, and which also determines the penalties to be imposed in case of infringement[251].

All these rules and requirements have the aim of providing information to consumers and learned intermediaries in order to enable them to make informed decisions, especially in relation to medicines' usage and risks of side-effect[252].

1.3.h Pharmacovigilance

Once the medicinal products are placed on the market following the rules designed to maintain the already recognised safety, quality and efficacy standards during the medicine's lifecycle, pharmaceuticals continue to be controlled with a series of activities known globally by the name of "pharmacovigilance". Considered to be a key public health function, this is more precisely the process of monitoring the safety of medicines, taking action to reduce the risks and the number of ADRs and detecting any change in the medicine's risk-benefit balance[253] through a proactive, transparent and patient-centred approach. The need for an effective pharmacovigilance system stems from the fact that although clinical trials are extremely closely controlled at each stage, some rare side effects may only appear after a long period of taking the medicine or once the product has been used by a large number of people or due to the aging of patients. This is why the main tools of pharmacovigilance consist of improving communication and data collection, increasing transparency and encouraging the active participation of patients and health professionals in order to be able to act promptly and effectively in response to any risks related to the safety or quality of medicinal products. The whole system is part of the difficult balance between the different needs at stake: on the one hand, to guarantee patients timely access to new

---

[249] Directive 2001/83/EC, Article 90.
[250] Ibid., Article 96.
[251] Ibid., Article 97.
[252] Pilgerstorfer, "EU Law", 168.
[253] Directive 2001/83/EC, Article 1(28d).

and advanced medicines; on the other, to find all the information necessary to ensure the safety, quality and the efficacy of the products.

The European pharmacovigilance system has a precise legal framework: the consolidated version of Regulation (EC) No. 726/2004 specifies the process with respect to Centrally Authorised Products (CAPs), whereas the consolidated version of the Community Code Directive deals with the system related to nationally authorised medicinal products (NAPs) or those authorised through the mutual recognition or the decentralised procedures[254]. As has been seen above, this legal framework has been (and will continue to be) subjected to some legislative developments, which consider scientific and technological advances and new needs while also correcting the errors and inefficiencies of the previous pharmacovigilance system. Indeed, the major reform of the medicines safety monitoring system took place at the urging of the European Commission which, since 2005, has introduced significant innovations, such as extensive public consultation and the sponsorship of independent studies, which led to the adoption of Directive 2010/84/EU and Regulation (EU) No. 1235/2010 that amended the aforementioned legislation.

In addition, Commission Implementing Regulation (EU) No. 520/2012[255] on the performance of pharmacovigilance activities describes operational details about certain aspects of pharmacovigilance to be respected by the marketing authorisation holders, the national competent authorities and the EMA.

Finally, after the withdrawal from the European market of the medicines containing benfluorex and with the aim of improving a system for the prompt notification and assessment of safety issues, the pharmacovigilance legislation was further amended with Directive 2012/26/EU and Regulation (EU) No. 1027/2012.

Moreover, still with regard to the context of the principles of generic good practice, the EMA has released good pharmacovigilance practice guidelines (GVP) in order to facilitate the performance of pharmacovigilance activities in the Union.

---

[254] Ibid., Articles 101-108b.

[255] Commission Implementing Regulation (EU) No. 520/2012 of 19 June 2012 on the performance of pharmacovigilance activities provided for in Regulation (EC) No. 726/2004 of the European Parliament and of the Council and Directive 2001/83/EC of the European Parliament and of the Council; 2012 O.J. (L 159) 5, https://eur-lex.europa.eu/LexUriServ/LexUriServ.do?uri=OJ:L:2012:159:0005:0025:EN:PDF

By going into more detail about the pharmacovigilance process, it can be discovered that the whole system is predisposed to a variety of activities to be carried out by a number of subjects, each of which has precise obligations and tasks. Many actors are directly involved in the entire pharmacovigilance system: patients, healthcare professionals, the EMA, the European Commission, the national competent authorities of the 31 countries of the European Economic Area (EEA), pharmaceutical companies and companies importing or distributing medicines.

In particular, healthcare professionals have to monitor the feedback received from their patients on any adverse reactions (ADRs) no later than 15 days following the receipt of the information[256]. Consequently, the web-based EudraVigilance system for managing and analysing information on suspected serious side effects and safety reports in general was created.

The holder of a marketing authorisation has to, *inter alia*, evaluate all information scientifically; consider options for risk minimisation and prevention and take appropriate measures as necessary; nominate a qualified person responsible for pharmacovigilance; perform a regular audit of his pharmacovigilance system; create a risk management system for each product; maintain a master file; monitor risks against the Risk Management Plan (RMP) and reassess the benefit-risk balance [257]. Obviously, the marketing authorisation holders have to record all suspected adverse reactions in the Union or in third countries which are brought to their attention and submit the information electronically to the EudraVigilance database within 15 days[258].

Moreover, Periodic Safety Update Reports (PSURs), containing summaries of the relevant data and their scientific evaluation, must be prepared and submitted to the Agency[259].

National competent authorities, marketing authorisation holders and the various sponsors can register on the EudraVigilance database in order to respect their legal obligations. The aim of the system is to protect the public from emerging safety issues by the continuous collection of relevant information about medicines available on the market in order to take precise action in response. If, for example, an issue with an authorised medicine occurs in more than one Member State, the same regulatory

---

256 Regulation (EC) No. 726/2004, Article 24.
257 Directive 2001/83/EC, Article 104.
258 Ibid., Article 107.
259 Ibid., Article 107b.

action and the same guidance is provided to all patients and healthcare professionals in all the European countries involved[260].

For their part, Member States, the EMA, and the European Commission are the main responsible parties for the implementation and operation of much of the pharmacovigilance legislation. In particular, each Member State shall designate a competent authority for the performance of the pharmacovigilance tasks[261], while the Commission may request Member States to participate, under the coordination of the Agency, in the international harmonisation and standardisation of technical measures to be adopted in the pharmacovigilance process[262]. Furthermore, the European Commission, which is the competent authority for centrally authorised medicines, shall regularly publish a report on the performance of pharmacovigilance tasks by the Member States[263] and the EMA[264] every three years[265].

The individual Member States of the EEA are the main responsible parties for the creation and the subsequent control of an effective pharmacovigilance system operating at a national level.

The Coordination Group for Mutual Recognition and Decentralised Procedures – Human (CMDh), composed of one representative per Member State, as its fundamental task has the aim of examining any questions related to the pharmacovigilance of medicines authorised following the mutual recognition or the decentralised procedures[266].

---

[260] European Medicines Agency, *The European regulatory system for medicines: A consistent approach to medicines regulation across the European Union*, EMA/716925/2016, 4, https://www.ema.europa.eu/documents/leaflet/european-regulatory-system-medicines-european-medicines-agency-consistent-approach-medicines_en.pdf.

[261] Directive 2001/83/EC, Article 101(3).

[262] Ibid., Article 101(4).

[263] Ibid., Article 108b.

[264] Regulation (EC) No. 726/2004, Article 29.

[265] The first and last report of the Commission was published on 8 August 2016 and analyses the pharmacovigilance-related activities of Member States and the European Medicines Agency concerning medicinal products for human use, focusing on the activities since the start of the operation of new legislation in 2012 until the end of 2014; see European Commission, *Pharmacovigilance related activities of Member States and the European Medicines Agency concerning medicinal products for human use (2012-2014)* (Report from the Commission, COM(2016) 498 final, 2016), https://ec.europa.eu/health/sites/health/files/files/pharmacovigilance/pharmacovigilance-report-2012-2014_en.pdf.

[266] Directive 2001/83/EC, Article 27(1.b).

By contrast, the EMA is in charge of the coordination of supervision activities and to provide public access to reports of suspected side effects for centrally-authorised medicines. In order to fulfil this assignment, the Agency has a particular committee dedicated to the safety of medicines for human use, the Pharmacovigilance Risk Assessment Committee (PRAC), which includes representatives of healthcare professionals and patients, associates appointed by the Member States and independent experts selected by the Commission. The Committee, effective since 2012, has the role of assessing all aspects of risk management of human medicines, including the detection, minimisation and communication of the risk of adverse reactions, designing the post-authorisation safety studies, and providing recommendations on questions on pharmacovigilance to the European medicines regulatory network. In addition, the PRAC may, if useful, hold public hearings during safety reviews of medicines intended to support the committee's decision-making process by providing perspectives, knowledge and insights about the use of medicines in clinical practice[267].

All these authorities do not carry out their tasks in a detached way from each other, but are part of a network in which the medicine regulatory authorities of the 31 EEA countries, the EMA and the European Commission closely collaborate to deal with any emerging problem in the interest of patients' access to safe and efficacious medicines.

In conclusion, it could be said that pharmacovigilance has evolved into a public health-oriented scientific system, characterised by a reactivity to new and emerging safety information and continual effectiveness monitoring in an environment of transparency and openness[268].

---

[267] European Medicines Agency, *European regulatory system.*

[268] Aniello Santoro et al., "Promoting and Protecting Public Health: How the European Union Pharmacovigilance System Works", *Drug Safety* 40, no. 10 (October 2017): 855-869, https://doi.org/10.1007/s40264-017-0572-8.

CHAPTER TWO

THE JURISPRUDENCE OF THE COURT OF JUSTICE OF THE EUROPEAN UNION

2.1 The Role of the CJEU in EU Health Law

As has already been underlined in the introduction, the EU's limited legal basis for the regulation of healthcare, in what has been called a "patchwork" of competences, has provoked a lack of legal certainty and various conflicts between national and European policies. Therefore, with the ultimate purpose of harmonising the different national health regulations and developing the single market of medicinal products, European institutions have mostly relied on their limited legislative competence in this field; juridical decisions; *ad hoc* created agencies and committees; the wide use of EU non-legislative tools; and technical guidelines.

As a matter of fact, health policies are closely related to national identities, causing, as a result, a high number of disputes in relation to any cross-border element correlated to healthcare. An important outcome of this phenomenon has been the emergence of the leading role of the Court of Justice of the European Union (CJEU)[269]. Through its "teleological" approach to the interpretation of EU law, and given the institutional constraints upon the European legislature, the Court has managed to set policy directions especially on the basis of atypical cases within the single market rules and, to some extent, competition law[270]. In this way, the Court has set crucial precedents in areas such as, for instance, patient mobility, the reimbursement of medical costs, the mutual recognition of already authorised pharmaceuticals, the intellectual property protection of

[269] Mossialos et al., *Health Systems Governance*, 15.

[270] Martin McKee and Elias Mossialos, "Health policy and European law: closing the gaps", *Public Health* 120, no. S1, (October 2006): 16-22, https://doi.org/10.1016/j.puhe.2006.07.008.

innovative and advanced medicines and, more recently, health solidarity and equality.

In particular, three heads of the CJEU's jurisdiction have been the most used ones in health-related disputes: applications for a judicial review of EU institutions' acts[271], Commission allegations of non-compliance with EU law by Member States[272], and preliminary references from national courts[273].

Within the preliminary reference system[274], which is the most significant one, the CJEU has the competence to give authoritative rulings on the validity and interpretation of EU law, where such interrogations are advanced before any national court or tribunal in the Member States. Moreover, because of the supremacy of EU law, the CJEU's authoritative decisions have the effect of making any national rules that are inconsistent with EU law inapplicable[275]. Thus, the internal relationship between courts determines the external relationship between the CJEU and other stakeholders, especially Member States' governments and national legislatures[276]. In this way, the Court has filled gaps that have been uncovered by legal disputes, reduced inconsistencies, and indirectly influenced national health policies by limiting Member States' specific competences in social matters and undermining the relative state territoriality.

For this and other reasons, the phenomenon of the CJEU developing EU health law has been the object of numerous criticisms such as, more generally, the unpredictability of law and the difficulty of determining the precise implications or the scope of individual rulings without legislative

---

[271] TFEU, Article 263.

[272] Ibid., Article 258.

[273] Ibid., Article 267.

[274] According to Article 267 TFEU, EU national courts may submit a referral to the CJEU concerning the interpretation of the Treaties or the validity of acts of the institutions, bodies or agencies of the Union when the decision on such questions is necessary to enable the national court to give judgement, or where the existing case law does not appear to give the necessary guidance to deal with a new legal situation. The national court which requested the preliminary ruling has to render judgement on the basis of the CJEU's decision. Moreover, given that the CJEU's judgement is a binding official interpretation of EU law, it must be applied to all Member States.

[275] See Case 6/64, Flaminio Costa v. ENEL, 1964 E.C.R. 01141, EU:C:1964:66.

[276] Clemens M. Rieder, "Courts and EU health law and policies", in *Research Handbook on EU Health Law and Policy,* eds. Tamara K. Hervey, Calum Alasdair Young and Louise E. Bishop (Cheltenham: Edward Elgar Publishing, 2017), 60-81.

guidance, and the fact that not all the relevant interests are taken into account when law is developed in this way[277].

In particular, however, the criticisms essentially concern the case law where the territorially closed national healthcare systems were challenged on the basis of the free movement of goods, services, persons and capital[278]. In this regard, there was a widespread worry that, in doing so, the Court adopted a market-oriented approach in the health field, which has a predominantly social character. This latter concern falls within the aforementioned constitutional asymmetry between the EU policies related to social protection and those related to market efficiency[279]. This is perhaps an oversimplification of the position, because the Court balances the place of welfare within the internal market by recognising that the internal market is not simply a deregulated economic space, but one where social and other non-economic dimensions are also embedded in market-correcting measures (and this especially after the Charter of Fundamental Rights of the European Union gained the same legal value as the EU Treaties with the entry into force of the Lisbon Treaty)[280].

Moreover, the Court was in fact doing exactly what it is mandated to do, that is, to interpret and apply a binding hard law. It does not create the rules per se, which is instead a Member State's responsibility within the European institutions. Therefore, if the governments of the Member States are unhappy with the Court's interpretation and application of the Treaties, can it not legitimately be asked whether they themselves are not at least in part responsible?

A consequence of Article 267 TFEU, which establishes the preliminary ruling procedure, is that the cooperation of national courts, which are responsible for determining the final judgments, is needed in order to concretely apply the CJEU's interpretations. But, in practice, national courts and tribunals have almost always respected the authority of the CJEU to give definitive interpretations of EU law[281]. This has happened even when the Court adopted methods of interpretation beyond the literal approach and thus created surprising rulings. Consequently, the influence

[277] Hervey and McHale, *European Union Health Law*, 138-144.
[278] Vollaard, Van de Bovenkamp and Martisen, *Making European*, 10.
[279] Scharpf, *European Social Model*, 645-670.
[280] Mossialos et al., *Health Systems Governance*, 29-30.
[281] Ibid.

of EU law into national legal orders has significantly improved, compared to that of other international organisations[282].

As a matter of fact, few legislative actions to reverse the CJEU's decisions have been adopted. The reason for this is that the numerous Member States are differently affected by the Court's decisions, therefore coalitions of support to change disputed legislations are extremely difficult to reach, resultantly entailing political passivity[283]. Hence, this inertia undermines the political will to effect change, and passivity is taken as a sign of tacit support[284].

Member States tried in different ways to exclude healthcare from the interference of the European Union's institutions but could not completely neutralise the CJEU's case law because of disagreements about the proper procedure to adopt[285].

Moreover, national attempts to reverse the Court's rulings are often impossible, given that most of the CJEU's decisions are based directly on the free movement principles laid down in the Treaties and thus could only be rolled back by changing these fundamental parts of the treaty[286]. Such failures have provided the European Commission with the opportunity to keep cross-border healthcare on the agenda by launching studies and discussion platforms, examining Member States' compliance with case law and codifying case law in subsequent EU legislation[287].

The inability of national governments to reject the Court's decisions through precise and agreed primary laws has been mitigated by the increasing national control and involvement in secondary legislation than was originally indicated by the Commission and case law. This facilitated the conclusion of a final compromise and ultimately confirmed the increasing role of the EU in the healthcare field[288].

Lastly, from another point of view, it could be said that CJEU rulings may indeed be seen like intrusions into national traditions and decision-making power, but, at the same time, this process enables EU law to

---

[282] Karen Alter, *The European Court's Political Power: Selected Essays* (Oxford: Oxford University Press, 2009).
[283] Mossialos et al., *Health Systems Governance*, 32.
[284] Alter, *European Court*.
[285] Hervey and Vanhercke, "Health care", 84-133.
[286] Ibid.
[287] Vollaard, Van de Bovenkamp and Martisen, *Making European*, 11.
[288] Ibid., 12.

protect individual rights against the potentially arbitrary decisions of national governments[289].

In conclusion, the above examination is a general discourse about the CJEU's jurisprudence as a legal source in the development of EU health law. It is however necessary to emphasise that there are some aspects of this matter where the CJEU's contribution is minimal and the key relevant sources are entirely based on hard law, which are at most reinforced by different instruments of soft law[290].

It is now necessary to go into more detail about the jurisprudence of the Court, dealing with cases more specifically related to pharmaceuticals.

2.2 The Jurisprudence of the CJEU on Pharmaceuticals

We have just seen the central role of the CJEU in its institutional task of interpreting and applying the provisions of EU health law, also creating, thanks to its remarkable jurisprudential work, innovative principles that were implemented into the subsequent legislation.

We are now going to analyse the case law of the Court specifically concerning pharmaceuticals. But, before going into detail about this topic, it is necessary to give a brief introduction to the approaches and philosophies adopted by the CJEU in the judgments it has pronounced in relation to this area.

Case law on pharmaceuticals is, for the most part, based on the free movement of medicinal products across borders within the European Community. In the 1950s and 1960s, each Member State usually protected the trade of medicines territorially. Where national healthcare policies and practices divide the European single market into different and numerous national ones, they are particularly susceptible to being challenged before national courts, and by extension, to the CJEU for violations of the free

---

[289] Renaud Dehousse, "Integration through law revisited: some thoughts on the juridification of the European political process", in *The Europeanisation of Law: The Legal Effects of European Integration,* ed. Francis Snyder (Oxford: Hart Publishing, 2000), 15-30.

[290] For instance, in practice, the EU's good laboratory practice and good clinical trials legislation is interpreted through the issuing of guidance notes, which, though non-binding in theory, have a binding effect in practice, because compliance with this guidance is normally required for studies used to support applications for clinical trials of marketing authorisations. See Hervey and McHale, *European Union Health Law*, 58.

movement rules. For this reason, since the beginning of the 1970s, the vast majority of litigants, who were and still are medicine producers or distributors, rely on EU law and the relative competent institutions to open up new community countries' markets in order to capitalise through economies of scale[291]. Therefore, for the most part, the CJEU's case law on health matters is based on free movement, non-discrimination, and negative integration in order to remove national obstacles to European market access[292].

This primarily market-oriented policy of the Court in relation to healthcare, which has a predominantly social character, has raised many criticisms, doubts and concerns. In this regard, the opinion expressed by Mr Advocate General Tesauro in Case C-60/89, Monteil and Samanni, is a clear and certainly glaring example:

> *In summarizing the events which gave rise to the present proceedings, I am unable to dispel the suspicion (...) that in disputes of this kind the role of the protagonist is played by Mercury, the god of commerce, rather than by, Hygeia, the goddess of health*[293].

These points of view, which certainly have an element of truth, do not take into account the fact that the European Community was initially created for the purpose of developing an area of free trade among the funding countries and all those who subsequently decided to join them in this "project". Therefore, the jurisdiction of the Court to apply and interpret European law especially concerns such market-oriented topics. In fact, medicines certainly have a great social connotation, but they still remain commercial goods and therefore cannot escape the free movement rules within the European single market.

Moreover, it is well known that an unfettered application of the deregulatory internal market law might pose significant threats to health within the Union, as well as other public interest objectives[294]. However, the free movement provisions in the TFEU do not act only as deregulatory mechanisms, nor do they confer rights without exceptions[295]. Indeed, the TFEU itself contains some specific exceptions to the general free

---

[291] Hervey and McHale, *European Union Health Law*, 98.
[292] Mossialos et al., *Health Systems Governance*, 11.
[293] Case C-60/89, Criminal proceedings against Jean Monteil and Daniel Samanni, 1991 E.C.R. I-01547, Opinion of AG Tesauro, para 1.
[294] Hervey and Vanhercke, "Health care", 95-98.
[295] Ibid.

movement rules, which do not preclude restrictions on imports and exports of goods justified on the grounds of

> *(...) public morality, public policy or public security; the protection of health and life of humans, animals or plants; the protection of national treasures possessing artistic, historic or archaeological value; or the protection of industrial and commercial property*[296].

Furthermore, in its jurisprudential work, the Court recognised that non-discriminatory restrictions on free movement rules are justified in pursuance of an "objective public interest"[297], such as consumer protection. *Exempli gratia*, this resolution policy based on consumer protection is particularly evident in a series of cases[298] brought to the attention of the Court, which was called to pronounce its ruling on the correct interpretation of the definition of medicine contained in the relevant European legislation (especially Directive 65/65/EEC). In particular, *inter alia*, in its judgment of the Delattre Case[299], there was the first jurisprudential recognition of the so-called principle of prevalence of the pharmaceutical discipline with respect to products that could hardly be identifiable as such: if there are doubts about the product category (for example, cosmetics, vitamins or food supplements) of the good in the case under examination, this latter must be considered a medicine and so the most rigorous discipline must be applied (such an orientation was subsequently codified in Directive 2004/27/EC). This indicates the consistency of the legislators and the judges in recognising, where necessary, the pre-eminence of the right to health protection over the free

---

[296] TFEU, Article 36.

[297] See, for example, Case 33/74, Johannes Henricus Maria van Binsbergen v. Bestuur van de Bedrijfsvereniging voor de Metaalnijverheid, 1974 E.C.R. 01299, ECLI:EU:C:1974:131; Case 71/76, Jean Thieffry v. Conseil de l'ordre des avocats à la cour de Paris, 1977 E.C.R. 00765, ECLI:EU:C:1977:65; Case C-384/93, Alpine Investments BV v. Minister van Financiën, 1995 E.C.R. I-01141, ECLI:EU:C:1995:126.

[298] Case 227/82, Criminal proceedings against Leendert van Bennekom, 1983 E.C.R. 03883, ECLI:EU:C:1983:354; Case C-369/88, Criminal proceedings against Jean-Marie Delattre, 1991 E.C.R. I-01487, ECLI:EU:C:1991:137; Case C-219/91, Criminal proceedings against Johannes Stephanus Wilhelmus Ter Voort, 1992 E.C.R. I-05485, ECLI:EU:C:1992:414; Case C-319/05, Commission of the European Communities v. Federal Republic of Germany, 2007 E.C.R. I-09811, ECLI:EU:C:2007:678.

[299] Case C-369/88, *Delattre*.

movement of goods[300]. Furthermore, in the Ter Voort Case[301], the Court once again affirmed that the primary interest to be safeguarded is the protection of consumers and their health.

However, more generally, in the Court's judgments the collective public health imperatives are much more prominent than the individual consumer protection frame[302]. This further demonstrates that the Court is sensitive to the potentially devastating application of internal market law in social contexts, including healthcare[303]. Of course, there must be a legitimate public interest, which should be not disproportionate to the distortion of the internal market involved, and finally it may not be a 'purely economic' aim. Nevertheless, the structure of the Court's case law is flexible, leaving the possibility of introducing further justifications for national policies and practices[304].

In this regard, it is important to note an additional, relatively recent approach adopted by the CJEU, which held in several cases that barriers to trade in the internal market can be justified by the need for Member States to secure the financial stability of their health systems[305]. The financial strength of national health services as a barrier to the free movement of goods has its origins in the Roussel Case[306], finding its subsequent consecration in the Duphar Case[307] and was later repeatedly invoked (especially in the jurisprudence concerning cross-border patient mobility from the Decker Case[308] onwards). The Court, in its *Decker* Case judgment, expressed that

> *It must be recalled that aims of a purely economic nature cannot justify a barrier to the fundamental principle of the free movement of goods. However, it cannot be excluded that the risk of seriously undermining the*

---

[300] Marco Inglese, "*Unione Europea e sanità*" (PhD diss., Università di Bologna, 2014), 64.
[301] Case C-219/91, *Ter Voort*.
[302] Hervey and McHale, *European Union Health Law*, 98.
[303] Hervey and Vanhercke, "Health care", 95-98.
[304] Ibid., 98.
[305] Case 181/82, Roussel Laboratoria BV and others v. État néerlandais, 1983 E.C.R. 03849, ECLI:EU:C:1983:352; Case C-249/88, Commission of the European Communities v. Kingdom of Belgium, 1991 E.C.R. I-01275, ECLI:EU:C:1991:21.
[306] Case 181/82, *Roussel*.
[307] Case 238/82, Duphar BV and others v. The Netherlands State, 1984 E.C.R. 00523, ECLI:EU:C:1984:45.
[308] Case C-120/95, *Decker*.

> *financial balance of the social security system may constitute an overriding reason in the general interest capable of justifying a barrier of that kind*[309].

This last example is a demonstration of the evolving nature of the Court's jurisprudence, which not only interprets the existing EU legislation broadly in order to guarantee greater protection for citizens, but also, and above all, demonstrates the tendency to adapt its case law to the new needs that may arise in the European economic-social panorama.

As a further demonstration of this jurisprudential propensity, the recent increase of healthcare-related cases raised on the basis of alleged violations of fundamental rights should be noted.

The European Union has not traditionally been a fundamental rights body, but due to Treaty amendments and institutional developments, this body of law has become a substantial part of EU law, standing among the founding values of the Union as a whole[310]. Indeed, with the entering into force of the Lisbon Treaty in 2009, the Charter of Fundamental Rights of the European Union (CFREU) became legally binding with the same legal values of the Treaties[311]. From that moment on, a series of substantial changes modified the EU fundamental rights architecture. In this way, any contemporary assessment of EU health law and policy requires an understanding of the effects of fundamental rights jurisprudence, as well as the broader conceptualisation of health as a fundamental right[312]. Consequently, the initial constitutional asymmetry, so heavily criticised, has been attenuated over time until its almost complete disappearance. Moreover, fundamental rights influence access to healthcare and conceptualise public health as a fundamental right, reinforcing, in this way, the existing limitations on free movement. At the moment, however, the CFREU's impact on EU health law has not been well documented, and many effects may yet emerge especially in relation to the pharmaceutical area. Nevertheless, it is interesting to discuss this new source of law and

---

309 Ibid., para 39.
310 TEU, Article 2.
311 Ibid., Article 6.
312 Calum Alasdair Young, "Fundamental rights and EU health law and policy", in *Research Handbook on EU Health Law and Policy,* eds. Tamara K. Hervey, Calum Alasdair Young and Louise E. Bishop (Cheltenham: Edward Elgar Publishing, 2017), 82-83.

the related jurisprudential application to better understand the direction of travel of this particular field[313].

Finally, it should be noted that because the pharmaceutical industry's purchasing activities have been considerably subjected to control under EU competition law, this legal framework has also shaped the market and policies related to medicinal products, especially in terms of cost reductions, market structure and innovation[314]. The influence of competition law was also extended in sectors characterised by public interest and values thanks to the work of the CJEU, which, over time, has interpreted such provisions extensively[315]. It is therefore necessary also to analyse the Court's jurisprudence on cases brought to its attention by the pharmaceutical industry, which is repeatedly hit by antitrust rules.

In light of these general considerations, we will now proceed with the analysis of the most significant jurisprudential cases related to pharmaceuticals and treated by the CJEU, starting on the basis of the two regulatory frameworks that historically affected this sector in the most considerable way, namely the free movement of goods and competition law, before concluding with the recent jurisprudence based on fundamental rights.

2.2.a The Free Movement of Goods

According to Articles 34 and 35 TFEU, any quantitative restrictions on imports and exports respectively, or any measures having an equivalent effect between Member States, are prohibited. The CJEU, in its famous judgment pronounced in resolution of the Dassonville Case[316], specified the meaning of "equivalent effect" to quantitative restrictions as

---

313 Ibid., pp. 82-108.

314 Johan W. Van de Gronden and Catalin S. Rusu, "EU competition law and policy and health systems", in *Research Handbook on EU Health Law and Policy,* eds. Tamara K. Hervey, Calum Alasdair Young and Louise E. Bishop (Cheltenham: Edward Elgar Publishing, 2017), 267-290.

315 Wolf Sauter and Johan W. Van de Gronden, "State Aid, Services of General Economic Interest and Universal Service in Healthcare", *European Competition Law Review* 32, no. 12 (January 2011): 615-620.

316 Case 8/74, Procureur du Roi v. Benoît and Gustave Dassonville, 1974 E.C.R. 00837, ECLI:EU:C:1974:82.

(...) all trading rules enacted by Member States which are capable of hindering, directly or indirectly, actually or potentially, intra-Community trade.

The key point is that, in order to determine whether a measure corresponds to a restriction on an import/export, it should look merely to its effect on the market and not to its purpose. Additionally, as already noted, Article 36 TFEU sets an exhaustive list of explicit justifications for restricting the free movement of goods towards the EU internal market, taking care also to specify that

(...) such prohibitions or restrictions shall not, however, constitute a means of arbitrary discrimination or a disguised restriction on trade between Member States.

The Court undertook to interpret the provisions in question in its landmark decision of the Cassis de Dijon Case[317]. In this regard, it was stated that, under the principle of mutual recognition, a product lawfully saleable in one Member State should be freely marketable in another Member State. Nevertheless, the Court, knowing that important market failures might occur and that the financial sustainability of national systems could, in this way, be threatened, introduced the concept of "overriding reasons of public interest" to act in addition to the legitimate grounds of justification set out by Article 36 TFEU as a defence of the obstacle to free movement. Such reasons may only be invoked if restrictions to imports/exports have a non-discriminatory effect and are therefore equally applied to both domestic and foreign products. The list of the overriding reasons of public interest, which initially included, for example, the effectiveness of fiscal supervision, the protection of public health, the fairness of commercial transactions and the defence of the consumer, has grown over time thanks to the Court's case law.

Moreover, according to the proportionality principle[318], if a restriction was imposed to achieve a legitimate public health goal, it must be proportionated to the goal it pursues and it must use the least restrictive means to achieve it[319]. The rule imposed by this principle requires that

---

[317] Case 120/78, Rewe-Zentral AG v. Bundesmonopolverwaltung für Branntwein, 1979 E.C.R. 00649, ECLI:EU:C:1979:42.

[318] According to Article 5 TEU, the proportionality principle limits the exercise of the powers of the European Union institutions to what is necessary to achieve the objectives of the Treaties.

[319] McKee, Hervey and Gilmore, "Public Health Policies", 249-250.

even if a restriction or measure of equivalent effect is justifiable, this does not automatically validate its application to every specific situation. In this way, the true challenge rests not so much in the identification of the public interest objectives, but rather in providing proof that the measure in question is proportionate to its aim and that a less restrictive alternative is not plausible. As a consequence, Member States face a relatively high burden of proof due to the fact that proving what would hypothetically occur without the restriction is very laborious[320].

In its subsequent case law, the Court further expanded the scope of these principles and specified additional elements to be applied to particular concrete cases. For instance, restrictions are permitted even where there is just a genuine doubt about the risk to health[321]. In contrast, restrictions viewed primarily as obstacles to trade, even when they might possibly be justified on the grounds of public health, are not allowed[322]. Finally, the free movement rules come into play even if the regulatory measure that is under scrutiny lacks a specific potential cross-border element[323].

It is also important to note, for the purpose of the following analysis, that individuals may bring proceedings before their national courts in order to fight against national laws which provide for any unjustified restrictions to the freedom of movement. In particular, in relation to the healthcare sector, where national rules inhibit consumer choice, patients can rely upon provisions of EU law, which grant directly effective[324] rights to

---

320 Mossialos et al., *Health Systems Governance*, 65-66.

321 See, for example, Case 53/80, Officier van justitie v. Koninklijke Kassfabriek Eyssen BV, 1981 E.C.R. 00409, ECLI:EU:C:1981:35.

322 See, for example, Case 40/82, Commission of the European Communities v. United Kingdom of Great Britain and Northern Ireland, 1984 E.C.R. 00283, ECLI:EU:C:1984:33.

323 Case C-55/94, Reinhard Gebhard v. Consiglio dell'Ordine degli Avvocati e Procuratori di Milano, 1995 E.C.R. I-04165, ECLI:EU:C:1995:411; Case C-108/96, Criminal proceedings against Dennis Mac Quen, Derek Pouton, Carla Godts, Youssef Antoun and Grandvision Belgium SA, being civilly liable, intervener: Union professionnelle belge des médecins spécialistes en ophtalmologie et chirurgie oculaire, 2001 E.C.R. I-00837, ECLI:EU:C:2001:67; and Case C-294/00, Deutsche Paracelsus Schulen für Naturheilverfahren GmbH v. Kurt Gräbner, 2002 E.C.R. I-06515, ECLI:EU:C:2002:442.

324 Case 26/62, NV Algemene Transport-en Expeditie Onderneming van Gend & Loos v. Netherlands Inland Revenue Administration, 1963 E.C.R. 00001, EU:C:1963:1; Case 2/74, Jean Reyners v. Belgian State, 1974 E.C.R. 00631,

individuals facing unjustified restrictions to free movement in order to challenge national barriers to trade. Indeed, according to the principle of the primacy of European Union law, national courts must apply the Treaty provisions as a priority over national law.

In light of these broad considerations necessary to understand the application mechanisms of the free movement of goods, which are not only limited to the explicit treaty provisions but also to the extensive interpretations implemented by the CJEU, we turn now to look at a recent case that is perfectly exemplary of the principles and jurisprudential reasoning just discussed.

In the case C-148/15[325], the CJEU ruled that the German law on medicinal products, in its original version and the following amendment, which provided for a system of fixed prices for the sale by pharmacies of prescription-only medicinal products, constituted an infringement of EU law.

However, let us first go over the facts. The German self-help organisation Deutsche Parkinson Vereinigung eV (DPV), which seeks to improve the lives of patients suffering from Parkinson's disease, agreed with the Dutch mail-order pharmacy DocMorris to award DPV's members with a bonus when purchasing prescription-only medicinal products for Parkinson's disease from DocMorris.

A German association for protection against unfair competition started a proceeding before the Regional Court of Düsseldorf, which allowed the application, ordering that the bonus system infringed the German legislation that provides for a fixed-price system for the supply of prescription-only medicinal products by pharmacies. The Court of first instance upheld the claim and ordered DPV not to recommend the challenged bonus system. Subsequently, DPV appealed to the Higher Regional Court of Düsseldorf, which, in turn, referred the matter to the Court of Justice, asking whether this fixed-price system is compatible with the free movement of goods.

The CJEU ruled that:

> *Article 34 TFEU must be interpreted as meaning that national legislation, which provides for a system of fixed prices for the sale by pharmacies of*

EU:C:1974:68; Case 41/74, Yvonne van Duyn v. Home Office, 1974 E.C.R. 01337, EU:C:1974:133; Case 43/75, Gabrielle Defrenne v. Société anonyme belge de navigation aérienne Sabena, 1976 E.C.R. 00455, EU:C:1976:5.

[325] Case C-148/15, Deutsche Parkinson Vereinigung eV v. Zentrale zur Bekämpfung unlauteren Wettbewerbs eV, ECLI:EU:C:2016:776.

prescription-only medicinal products, constitutes a measure having equivalent effect to a quantitative restriction on imports, within the meaning of that article, since that legislation has a greater impact (...) in other Member States than (...) within the national territory[326].

Indeed, given that mail-order pharmacies cannot provide patients with individually-tailored services as traditional pharmacies do, price competition is capable of providing a more important competitive factor for mail-order pharmacies, since price competition lays the basis for their potential access to the German market.

Subsequently, the CJEU assessed whether the applicant provided the necessary supporting evidence to demonstrate that the German price fixing regime could be considered a legitimate justification to obstruct the free movement of goods, and, in particular, as a system for the protection of public health pursuant to Article 36 TFEU. Indeed,

(...) the reasons which may be invoked by a Member State by way of justification must thus be accompanied by an analysis of the appropriateness and proportionality of the measure adopted by that State, and by specific evidence substantiating its arguments[327].

The Court specified that:

Article 36 TFEU must be interpreted as meaning that such national legislation (...) cannot be justified on grounds of the protection of health and life of humans, inasmuch as that legislation is not appropriate for attaining the objectives pursued[328].

Hence, since it was not demonstrated that fixed prices ensured a better geographical distribution of traditional pharmacies in Germany, or that, in the absence of this system, mail-order pharmacies would compete in terms of price in a way that essential services could no longer be guaranteed, especially in rural areas, due to a consequential fall in the number of dispensing pharmacies, the legislation at issue could not be considered an appropriate means by which to attain the protection of health and life of humans by ensuring a safe and high-quality supply of pharmaceuticals.

The Court also noted that, faced with price competition from mail-order pharmacies, traditional pharmacies will even be encouraged to increase the development of certain activities in the general interest, and

---

[326] Ibid., para 27.
[327] Ibid., para 35.
[328] Ibid., para 46.

also to provide the benefit to patients of more attractive prices than those currently imposed.

Obviously, the judgment implies that all Member States must ensure that any national provisions concerning fixed prices on prescription-only medicinal products comply with this decision of the CJEU.

It may be that the principles of free movement collide with other rights guaranteed at European level, thus creating the need to establish the hierarchical relationship between them. This is exactly what happened between the rules of the free movement of goods and Intellectual Property Rights (IPR). In particular, parallel importers have relied on EU law to challenge the exercise of IPR by the original manufacturers of medicines, which, on their part, seek to rely on them in order to prevent the parallel import of pharmaceuticals. This happens because the establishment of pharmaceutical prices remain the Member States' competence. In this way, price differences are created between EU countries, which are sufficiently great to encourage parallel importers to buy and subsequently move pharmaceuticals from one Member State in which they are cheaper into another in which they are more expensive in order to profit from the price difference[329].

EU law protects and supports parallel imports because they may increase consumer welfare thanks to the correlated tendency of reducing products' prices and, in general, of being an instrument for achieving and maintaining the single market.

According to Article 345 TFEU:

> *The Treaties shall in no way prejudice the rules in the Member States governing the system of property ownership.*

More precisely, in the exhaustive list of explicit justifications for restricting the free movement of goods towards the Union provided by Article 36 TFEU, there is also the protection of industrial and commercial property. But, nevertheless, in the 1970s, the CJEU held that[330], once the IPR have been "exhausted" by the product being placed on the market in one Member State, restrictions on parallel imports of goods are in principle an unjustified breach of the free movement of goods[331].

---

329 Hervey and McHale, *European Union Health Law*, 109.
330 Case 15/74, Centrafarm BV and Adriaan de Peijper v. Sterling Drug Inc, 1974 E.C.R. 01147, ECLI:EU:C:1974:114; and Case 16/74, Centrafarm BV and Adriaan de Peijper v. Winthrop BV, 1974 E.C.R. 01183, ECLI:EU:C:1974:115.
331 Hervey and McHale, *European Union Health Law*, 109.

According to the exhaustion principle, which was created in order to eliminate any risk of potential artificial divisions within the internal market, the owner of an IPR could not invoke it to prevent the importation and sale of a medicinal product already placed on the market with his consent in another Member State[332]. In this regard, the CJEU further specified that an IPR holder who trades his product in two different Member States cannot prevent arbitrage between the two local markets, despite the differences in intellectual property protection in the two countries[333]. Thus, exhaustion applies only upon the first sale anywhere in the EU[334].

However, like almost every principle, exhaustion is characterised by significant limitations. Most importantly, the CJEU rejected the idea of an international exhaustion, extending the principle only to countries who are members of the internal market[335]. Furthermore, community exhaustion does not apply in relation to cases where the products are sold in a Member State under a compulsory license[336]. Consequently, so long as the manufacturer has voluntarily placed the product on the market, parallel imports within the EU territory are allowed, despite the existence of national intellectual property regimes and price controls[337].

Finally, even if the conditions for the exhaustion of rights are fulfilled, in exceptional cases, intellectual property rights owners can prevent the resale of goods, for example when trademark protected goods are altered, de-packaged or repackaged. In this regard, both the European legislator and the CJEU felt the need to regulate the trademarks in internal market law. Parallel importers must very often repackage medicinal products in order to sell them efficiently in other Member States, giving particular

[332] Leigh Hancher, "The European Community dimension: coordinating divergence", in *Regulating pharmaceuticals in Europe: striving for efficiency, equity and quality,* eds. Elias Mossialos, Monique Mrazek and Tom Walley (Maidenhead: Open University Press, 2004), 65.

[333] Case 187/80, Merck & Co. Inc. v. Stephar BV and Petrus Stephanus Exler, 1981 E.C.R. 02063, ECLI:EU:C:1981:180.

[334] Mattias Ganslandt, Keith Maskus, "Parallel Imports of Pharmaceutical Products in the European Union" (Policy Research Working Paper Series, No. 2630, The World Bank, 2011), 2-3, https://EconPapers.repec.org/RePEc:wbk:wbrwps:2630.

[335] Case 51/75, EMI Records Limited v. CBS United Kingdom Limited, 1976 E.C.R. 00811, ECLI:EU:C:1976:85; Case C-355/96, Silhouette International Schmied GmbH & Co. KG v. Hartlauer Handelsgesellschaft mbH, 1998 E.C.R. I-04799, ECLI:EU:C:1998:374.

[336] Case 19/84, Pharmon BV v. Hoechst AG, 1985 E.C.R. 02281, ECLI:EU: C:1985:304.

[337] Ganslandt and Maskus, "Parallel Imports", 2-3.

attention to consumer preferences. They also re-affix the trademark on the new packaging to show medicines' properties. The CJEU in its judgement of the Bristol-Myers Squibb case[338] specified the conditions under which a parallel importer can place an authentic trademark in the repackaging of a medicinal product already placed on the market in one Member State. When the conditions, which essentially are the respect of the notification requirements, the identification of the original manufacturer and package and that the repackaging would not affect the product and reputation of the trademark holder, are fulfilled, the trademark rights are exhausted[339].

Numerous controversies have arisen regarding parallel imports, especially in the medicinal products field. Indeed, it is a common practice for pharmaceutical companies to restrict the parallel trade of their products in order to combat the consequential reduction in their profits. This trend has been significantly fought by the competent European institutions, partly because the practices of pharmaceutical companies aiming to restrict the parallel trade of medicines in the Union not only violate the principles of the free movement of goods, but also because they can infringe competition law.

2.2.b Competition Law

Alongside the provisions on free movement, the European legislator created a system which seeks to ensure that competition within the internal market is not distorted. The role of competition law in maintaining the efficiency of the single market, especially through the protection of consumer welfare, has made this sector one of the most important policy areas in the Union.

This legislative branch is based, at the European Union level, on the provisions laid down in Articles 101–9 TFEU, which have been implemented over time by other sectorial legislations, the Commission's administrative decisions and the jurisprudence of the CJEU. In particular, the Treaty's provisions prohibit anti-competitive agreements between firms[340], abuse of a dominant position[341], and state aids to industry that

---

338 Case Joined Cases C-427/93, C-429/93 and C-436/93, Bristol-Myers Squibb v Paranova A/S (C-427/93) and C. H. Boehringer Sohn, Boehringer Ingelheim KG and Boehringer Ingelheim A/S v Paranova A/S (C-429/93) and Bayer Aktiengesellschaft and Bayer Danmark A/S v Paranova A/S (C-436/93), 1996 E.C.R. I-03457, ECI:EU:C:1996:282.

339 Hervey and McHale, *European Union Health Law*, 109-10.

340 TFEU, Article 101.

distort fair competition[342]. As with the free movement rules, in principle, the mere involvement in the market of the national healthcare system is not itself sufficient to remove it from the application of EU competition law. But, since the 1950s, there has been a specific legal exemption for

> *(...) undertakings entrusted with the operation of services of general economic interest,*

to the extent that the application of EU competition law would prevent such firms from carrying out the particular tasks entrusted to them[343]. As a consequence, this also being the case for national healthcare systems, such an exception to EU competition law may apply additionally to them[344].

By contrast with healthcare more generally, the antitrust rules have been applied extensively in the pharmaceuticals sector especially because of its intrinsic continuous fight between innovation and cost control. In particular, three types of cases about the blocking of parallel imports, the abuse of procedure and pay for delay are typical in this sector[345]. All three types of cases regard the IPR of the original manufacturer, while the last two concern the fight faced by the IPR owner against generics which can be placed on the market at a lower price compared to the original medicine, but only once intellectual property protection is exhausted[346].

Moreover, it is important to remember that EU competition law is also enforced by national competition authorities, which brought a lot of cases to the European competent institutions involving the pharmaceutical industry with the further aim of enhancing their national health systems[347].

In the previous paragraph, we saw, *inter alia*, in which ways and the reasons why the pharmaceutical industry tries to block parallel trade to protect the price differentiation of medicines. Any behaviour aimed at restricting parallel trade can be also a potential breach of EU competition law. The Commission imposed numerous sanctions on different pharmaceutical firms, which, through violations of Article 101 and 102

---

341 Ibid., Article 102.

342 Ibid., Article 107.

343 Ibid., Article 106(2).

344 Hervey and Vanhercke, "Health care", 101-102.

345 Leigh Hancher and Wolf Sauter, "A dose of competition: EU antitrust law in the pharmaceuticals sector", *Journal of Antitrust Enforcement* 4, no. 2 (October 2016): 381-410, https://doi.org/10.1093/jaenfo/jnw001.

346 Guy and Sauter, "History", 22-23.

347 Hervey and McHale, *European Union Health Law*, 278.

TFEU, restricted parallel trade with anti-competitive conducts, such as dual pricing practices or export controls[348]. In this regard, it is useful to remember two exemplary cases.

The first one[349] concerned an alleged violation of Article 101 TFEU by the British pharmaceutical company GlaxoSmithKline (hereinafter GSK), accused by the Commission of blocking parallel trade through its dual-pricing system. Indeed, charging different prices to distributors depending on the intended destination of pharmaceuticals may integrate an anti-competition practice. As a matter of fact, the Commission found that GlaxoWellcome SA (GW), a subsidiary of GSK, provided for dual pricing for supplies in Spain, with higher prices for exports of its medicines in order to bypass the lower prices of the domestic resale of their reimbursable drugs imposed by the Spanish regulation of its national market. The Commission found, in 2001, that GSK had violated Article 101(1) TFEU. However, GSK appealed to the CJEU, which, in 2009, held that such a dual pricing system did constitute a restriction of competition, but that it could benefit from the exemption set out in Article 101(3)[350] TFEU because the benefits of the agreement outweighed the disadvantages. The Court, therefore, concluded that the Commission had been wrong to reject GSK's arguments in favour of Article 101(3)

---

[348] Lazaros Grigorios Grigoriadis, "The Application of EU Competition Law in the Pharmaceutical Sector: The Case of Parallel Trade", *European Business Law Review* 25, no. 1 (2014): 141-201, https://ssrn.com/abstract=2206244.

[349] Joined Cases C-501/06 P, C-513/06 P, C-515/06 P and C-519/06 P, GlaxoSmithKline Services Unlimited v. Commission of the European Communities (C-501/06 P) and Commission of the European Communities v. GlaxoSmithKline Services Unlimited (C-513/06 P) and European Association of Euro Pharmaceutical Companies (EAEPC) v. Commission of the European Communities (C-515/06 P) and Asociación de exportadores españoles de productos farmacéuticos (Aseprofar) v. Commission of the European Communities (C-519/06 P), 2009 E.C.R. I-09291, ECLI:EU:C:2009:610.

[350] Article 101(3) TFEU provides that the prohibition contained in Article 101(1) TFEU (which prohibits all agreements between undertakings, decisions by associations of undertakings and concerted practices which may affect trade between EU Member States and which have as their object or effect the prevention, restriction or distortion of competition) may be declared inapplicable in the case of agreements which contribute to improving the production or distribution of goods or to promoting technical or economic progress, while allowing consumers a fair share of the resulting benefits, and which do not impose restrictions which are not indispensable to the attainment of these objectives and do not afford such undertakings the possibility of eliminating competition in respect of a substantial part of the products concerned.

exemptions concerning the strong levels of pharmaceutical sector competition of innovation, the need for sufficient levels of profitability for R&D investment, and the need for such profits to be generated globally despite the significant differences between Member States' health systems and price controls. Therefore, the CJEU annulled the Commission's rejection of GSK's Article 101(3) application.

The second case[351] still concerned behaviour that hindered parallel trade, but this time it was implemented through an abuse of a dominant position[352]. In summary, the case refers to various proceedings brought by some pharmaceutical wholesalers against the Greek subsidiary of GSK. In particular, the object of the case was the practice of GSK of stopping the supply of three prescription-only medicines to wholesalers in Greece (where pharmaceuticals have lower prices) apparently in order to prevent parallel exports to Member States charging higher prices for GSK's medicinal products at issue. The CJEU concluded that, under Article 102 TFEU, an undertaking with a dominant position in a relevant market for pharmaceutical products, which is the case for GSK, abuses its position when it refuses to meet ordinary orders from wholesalers in order to stop parallel exports to other Member States carried out by such wholesalers. Moreover, the Court concluded that:

> *It is for the national court to ascertain whether the orders are ordinary in the light of both the size of those orders in relation to the requirements of the market in the first Member State and the previous business relations between that undertaking and the wholesalers concerned*[353].

Obviously, everything fits into the optic, repeatedly referred to in the CJEU's jurisprudence[354], that a company must be entitled to take reasonable steps to protect its own commercial interests if these latter are attacked, but that such steps must be proportionate in relation to the threat to its commercial interests.

---

[351] Joined Cases C-468/06 to C-478/06, Sot. Lélos kai Sia EE and Others v. GlaxoSmithKline AEVE Farmakeftikon Proïonton, formerly Glaxowellcome AEVE, 2008 E.C.R. I-07139, ECLI:EU:C:2008:504.

[352] For the sake of clarity, and in a nutshell, an abuse of a dominant position occurs when a firm which has a position of strength in a certain marketplace exploits that position to adversely affect other companies.

[353] Ibid., para 77.

[354] Case 27/76, United Brands Company and United Brands Continentaal BV v. Commission of the European Communities, 1978 E.C.R. 00207, ECLI:EU: 1979:22.

The second type of cases, which involved the pharmaceutical sector and competitive law, concerns the "pay for delay" agreements under which companies corrupt generics producers so as to prevent them from entering the market (or delay their entry), despite the relevant patent being exhausted, at the expense of consumers, insurers or public purchasers[355]. The Commission began a sector-wide inquiry into such practices in 2008 and encouraged national competition authorities to enforce competition law in this regard[356]. The results were significant fines imposed by the Commission to different companies for those anticompetitive behaviours, all with the same aim of disengaging market entry by generics producers[357]. In particular, the Commission sanctioned companies which had entered into reverse patent settlement agreements with generics producers worth tens of millions of euros in order to guarantee the branded medicines companies that potential competitors would stay out of the market for the entire duration of the agreement[358]. Moreover, other fines were issued to companies which used a co-promotion agreement, under which some pharmaceutical firms paid a large sum of money to a generics company as long as this latter did not enter the market[359]. Finally, the Commission found an abuse of a dominant position perpetrated by an industry, which, *inter alia*, was accused of having induced reverse payment patent settlement agreements, having acquired scarce competing technologies, sent warning letters and created patent disputes in order to obstruct the entry into the market of a generic product of an own branded medicine[360].

In conclusion, it has been argued that such European investigations were also controversial because, for the first time, the EU authorities

---

[355] Guy and Sauter, "History", 22-23.

[356] European Commission, *Pharmaceutical Sector Inquiry* (Final Report, European Commission, 2009), http://ec.europa.eu/competition/sectors/pharmaceuticals/inquiry/staff_working_paper_part1.pdf.

[357] Olga Gurgula, "Restrictive Practices in Pharmaceutical Industry: Reverse Payment Agreements. Seeking for a Balance between Intellectual Property and Competition Law", *ICC Global Antitrust Review*, no. 5 (2012): 58-104, https://ssrn.com/abstract=2841884 or http://dx.doi.org/10.2139/ssrn.2841884.

[358] Case COMP/AT.39226, Lundbeck, Commission Decision, (June 19, 2013) (summary at 2015 O.J. (C 80) 19).

[359] Case COMP/AT.39685, Fentanyl, Commission Decision, (December 10, 2013) (summary at 2015 O.J. (C 142) 21).

[360] Case COMP/AT.39612, Perindopril (Servier), Commission Decision, (September 9, 2014).

found such exceptional settlements of patent disputes breached competition law[361].

The Commission also solicited Member States to create specific systems which would make generics available within national health systems automatically, but since the Union does not have the competence to request such behaviour, the mere fact of recommending it suggests that these forms of conduct of pharmaceutical companies may continue to be widespread[362].

The last type of cases to be analysed are those involving the abuse of procedure perpetrated by medicine producers which, exploiting the fragmented nature of the patent and market authorisation rules, strategically hindered generics companies from withdrawing information and production formats or corrupting national competent authorities in order to extend the protection of their own branded pharmaceuticals[363].

Exemplary of this last type of case is the AstraZeneca case. In particular, in 2005, the Commission imposed two fines on the British company AstraZeneca plc and its Swedish subsidiary AstraZeneca AB for having abused their dominant position[364]. The judgment was issued on the grounds that, first, AstraZeneca had provided misleading information to a number of patent offices and national courts to obtain supplementary protection certificates, and second, that the industry had used a selective de-registration of national marketing authorisations to block the entry of generics, despite being in line with the regulatory framework to de-register marketing authorisations. The Commission specified, for the first time, that the seemingly innocuous use of the regulatory system amounted to an abuse of a dominant position. AstraZeneca appealed to the Court of First Instance [365], which for its part, generally upheld the Commission's approach except in the part determining the start date of the abuse. AstraZeneca appealed, and the Commission cross-appealed on the

---

[361] Joaquin Almunia, "Commission fines Lundbeck and other pharma companies for delaying market entry of generic medicines: statement by Vice-President Almunia", European Commission, last updated February 19, 2018, http://europa.eu/rapid/press-release_SPEECH-13-553_en.htm.
[362] Hervey and McHale, *European Union Health Law*, 284.
[363] Hancher and Sauter, "A dose of competition".
[364] Case COMP/A.37.507/F3, AstraZeneca, Commission Decision, (June 15, 2005), 2006 O.J. (L 332) 24.
[365] Case T-321/05, AstraZeneca AB and AstraZeneca plc v. European Commission, 2010 E.C.R. II-02805, ECLI:EU:T:2010:266.

questions it had lost. The CJEU[366] rejected all the appeals, confirmed the abuse of dominant position and specified that an undertaking

> *(...) cannot use regulatory procedures in such a way as to prevent or make more difficult the entry of competitors on the market, in the absence of grounds relating to the defence of the legitimate interests of an undertaking engaged in competition on the merits or in the absence of objective justification*[367].

In conclusion, it could be said that the Commission, supported by the CJEU, has, in the most recent cases, expanded its post control investigations over certain practices implemented by the research based industry[368]. It is hoped that this recent trend, although necessary and justified, does not lead to an increasing reduction of the stimulus to innovation and research that distinguishes this sectorial industry, which would thus have enormous repercussions on everyone.

2.2.c Fundamental Rights

Fundamental rights have characterised the discourse of healthcare in international law and the national constitutions of European Member States, especially after the Nuremberg trials and the conclusion of the Universal Declaration of Human Rights[369]. Moreover, the importance of human rights in the healthcare sector is shown by the Council of Europe's Convention on Human Rights and Biomedicine[370], which indicates a series of fundamental rights that are essential in this area such as, *inter alia*, the consent to treatment[371], research[372], transplantation[373] and the right to information[374]. However, because several European countries did not

---

[366] Case C-457/10, AstraZeneca AB and AstraZeneca plc v. European Commission, ECLI:EU:C:2012:770.
[367] Ibid., para 134.
[368] Hancher, "EU Pharmaceuticals Market", 655.
[369] Jean McHale, "Fundamental rights and health care", in *Health systems Governance in Europe: The Role of European Union Law and Policy,* eds. Elias Mossialos et al. (New York: Cambridge University Press, 2010), 283.
[370] Convention for the protection of Human Rights and Dignity of the Human Being with Regard to Biology and Medicine: Convention on Human Rights and Biomedicine, Oviedo, April 4, 1997, *European Treaty Series* no. 164.
[371] Ibid., Articles 5-9.
[372] Ibid., Articles 15-18.
[373] Ibid., Articles 21-22.
[374] Ibid., Article 12.

ratify the above-mentioned Convention, the most influential human rights instrument of the Council of Europe has always been the European Convention on Human Rights and Fundamental Freedoms (ECHR). All the European Union Member States are also members of the Council of Europe; a fact that, thanks to the recognition of the application of human rights principles in healthcare and the conceptualisation of health as a fundamental right, has also led to an increasing protection of these rights at the national level. Furthermore, the CJEU stated that

> *(...) the respect for fundamental rights forms an integral part of the general principles of Community law protected by the Court of Justice*[375].

The crowning of these achievements was certainly the adoption of the Charter of Fundamental Rights of the European Union (CFREU) in 2000 and the recognition of its high legal value, the same as the Treaties'[376], with the entry into force of the Lisbon Treaty in 2009.

It must be specified that, even though the ECHR can influence EU health law and policy, the CFREU is the most prominent document for the recognition of fundamental rights and the relative Union jurisprudence[377]. In this regard, the most relevant provisions of the Charter in the healthcare sector are: Article 3, which refers to the integrity of the person and provides, *inter alia*, that, in the field of medicine and biology, the informed consent of the person must be respected; Article 21, which prohibits discriminations; and, most notably, Article 35, which states that:

> *Everyone has the right of access to preventive health care and the right to benefit from medical treatment under the conditions established by national laws and practices. A high level of human health protection shall be ensured in the definition and implementation of all Union policies and activities.*

The right to healthcare gave the Union an important instrument to expand its influence in this area despite the relative limited competence established in the Treaty. Moreover, the CJEU has the power to interpret[378] and review[379] EU acts and legislation of which fundamental rights constitutes a part. Thus, in conclusion, fundamental rights can be an

[375] Case 1/70, Internationale Handelsgesellschaft mbH v. Einfuhr-und Vorratsstelle für Getreide und Futtermittel, 1970 E.C.R. 01125, ECLI:EU:C:1970:114, para 4.
[376] TEU, Article 6(1).
[377] Young, "Fundamental rights", 87.
[378] TFEU, Article 267.
[379] TFEU, Article 263.

interpretative tool with potential policy-altering implications or something against which to test the practical safeguards of EU health regulations[380].

Having concluded the initial considerations, let us now turn our attention to the jurisprudential implications of the rights guaranteed by the CFREU and, in particular, those of Article 35.

The first paragraph of Article 35 CFREU contains an expression of individual entitlement to healthcare, which can be used to expand individual access to healthcare in general, and therefore also to pharmaceuticals, within the Union.

This was exactly what happened in the Stamatelaki Case[381]. As a brief review of the facts of the case, a Greek national, who had received treatment at a private hospital in the UK, was refused a reimbursement of the medical expenses by his Greek insurance institute. An appeal to the Administrative Court of First Instance of Athens was lodged against this decision, which referred to the Court of Justice for a preliminary ruling. What is important to note in this case is the opinion of the Advocate General, who pointed out that the right of citizens to healthcare, proclaimed in Article 35 CFREU, is becoming more and more important in the Community sphere and that

> *(...) this right is perceived as a personal entitlement unconnected to a person's relationship with social security and the Court of Justice cannot overlook that aspect*[382].

Declaring that health is a personal entitlement means that Member States may be responsible even for people who are not connected with a particular system (a form of supranational solidarity)[383]. Nevertheless, the CJEU refused to adopt this point of view, providing that a restriction to the free movement rules can be justified, *inter alia*, by the objective of maintaining a balanced medical and hospital service open to every person in order to ensure a high level of health protection. Moreover, the CJEU more explicitly rejected the above-mentioned position in the judgement of

[380] Young, "Fundamental rights", 97.

[381] Case C-444/05, Aikaterini Stamatelaki v. NPDD Organismos Asfaliseos Eleftheron Epangelmation (OAEE), 2007 E.C.R. I-03185, ECLI:EU:C:2007:231.

[382] Ibid., Opinion of AG Colomer, para 40, ECLI:EU:C:2007:24.

[383] Rieder, "Courts", 79.

another case[384] stating that EU citizenship does not guarantee that moving to another Member State

(...) is neutral with regard to social security[385].

The second paragraph of Article 35 CFREU, stating that a high level of health protection shall be ensured in all Union policies and activities (a repetition of the mainstreaming provision of Article 168 TFEU), led to the conceptualisation of public health as a fundamental right[386]. Since that moment, fundamental rights have been recalled in an increasing number of cases, given the fact that protection to health was already recognised as a legitimate defence for restrictions to free movement[387].

The CJEU considered the protection of public health as a justification to the infringement of free movement rules in the judgment of the joined cases Blanco Pérez and Chao Gómez[388] concerning the setting up of new pharmacies in the Spanish territory (and also recalled it in other cases[389]):

It is also apparent from Article 52(1) TFEU that the protection of public health can justify restrictions on the fundamental freedoms guaranteed by the Treaty, such as the freedom of establishment. More specifically, restrictions on the freedom of establishment may be justified by the objective of ensuring that the provision of medicinal products to the public is reliable and of good quality. The importance of that objective is confirmed by Article 168(1) TFEU and Article 35 of the Charter of Fundamental Rights of the European Union[390].

---

384 Case C-208/07, Petra von Chamier-Glisczinski v. Deutsche Angestellten-Krankenkasse, 2009 E.C.R. I-06095, ECLI:EU:C:2009:455.

385 Ibid., para 85

386 Young, "Fundamental rights", 102.

387 See, for example, Case 174/82, Criminal proceedings against Sandoz BV, 1983 E.C.R. 02445, ECLI:EU:C:1983:213.

388 Joined Cases C-570/07 and 571/07, José Manuel Blanco Pérez and María del Pilar Chao Gómez v. Consejería de Salud y Servicios Sanitarios (C-570/07) and Principado de Asturias (C-571/07), 2010 E.C.R. I-04629, ECLI:EU:C:2010:300.

389 Case C-84/11, Marja-Liisa Susisalo and Others, ECLI:EU:C:2012:374; Joined Case C-159/12 to 161/12, Alessandra Venturini v. ASL Varese and Others Maria Rosa Gramegna v. ASL Lodi and Others and Anna Muzzio v. ASL Pavia and Others, ECLI:EU:C:2013:791; Case C-28/09, European Commission v. Republic of Austria, 2011 E.C.R. I-13525, ECLI:EU:C:2011:854; Case C-528/13, Geoffrey Léger v. Ministre des Affaires sociales, de la Santé et des Droits des femmes and Etablissement français du sang, ECLI:EU:C:2015:288.

390 Joined Cases C-570/07 and 571/07, *Blanco Pérez*, para 63 to 65.

Obviously, the restrictions to the Treaty's freedoms, even if justified, must be further subjected to the proportionality test.

The more a justification is based on universally recognised fundamental rights, the less it will be necessary to excuse its protection, even for the most serious violations of the freedoms guaranteed by the Treaties. As a consequence, the more frequently this logic is used in the jurisprudence, the more importance the CFREU will gain[391]. This could further lead to a greater shift in the balance between the social right to health and the traditionally economic reasons given in EU internal market cases[392].

Nevertheless, it should be noted that this judicial logic also has the potential to alter the behaviour of other actors, such as governments, so that, in this way, who would be more inclined to further restrict market freedoms using the above-mentioned justifications. Conversely, applicants will hardly challenge health regulations on market grounds knowing that the CJEU will be less inclined to favour their position[393]. Moreover, the enforceability of rights is more plausibly used against EU institutions than against national authorities[394]. This is a risk that the Court does not intend to run. Therefore, in practice, it seems improbable that fundamental rights and the use of the EU Charter will have a radical impact on EU health law and policy. This direction of travel is further supported by four reasons. First, the generality of certain concepts, such as dignity or even the right to healthcare, makes fundamental rights particularly difficult to enforce. Second, it is extremely arduous to create a uniform EU dimension to fundamental human rights given the differing national religious, cultural and ethical approaches to certain related questions (think, for example, about abortion or euthanasia). Third, the CFREU contains ambiguity about situations where human rights conflict, and does not specify how to prioritise one right instead of another. Fourth, the competences of EU institutions limit the scope of the CFREU[395].

Because of all these practical difficulties, it is much more likely that the CFREU will

[391] Young, "Fundamental rights", 103.
[392] Ibid., p. 105.
[393] Ibid., p. 106.
[394] McHale, "Fundamental rights", 314.
[395] Ibid., pp. 312-314.

(...) function as a source of values and norms ... to influence the interpretation of EU legislative and other measures and to feed into policy-making and into EU activities more generally[396].

Moreover, the provisions of the Charter, elaborated through the work of the Fundamental Rights Agency (FRA), may serve EU institutions and Member States to develop new forms of governance in the context of healthcare[397].

[396] Sandra Freedman, "Transformation or dilution: fundamental rights in the EU social space", *European Law Journal* 12, no. 1 (January 2006): 41, https://doi.org/10.1111/j.1468-0386.2006.00306.x.
[397] Ibid.

CHAPTER THREE

EUROPEAN UNION SOFT LAW

Given the patchwork of the European health law in general, the difficulties in overcoming the Member States' differences and the growing need for greater collaboration across jurisdictions, European Union policy-makers have tried to reach their policy goals through alternative approaches[398], which can be summarised with the term "soft law" (also known as "new governance," "soft governance," or "experimental governance"). In particular, such forms of governance were mainly developed from the 1990s to the late 2000s, especially for the purpose of facilitating and improving the integration and harmonisation of European Union health policy within the more rigid framework of EU law[399].

The term "soft" condenses a variety of processes, approaches and systems that differ from the traditional hard law instruments and that are not reducible to the hierarchical command-and-control model[400]. The complete picture of the system and its *raison d'être* was brilliantly outlined in this way:

> *Instead of a top-down, hierarchical rule-based system where failures to adhere are sanctioned, or unregulated market-based approaches, the new governance school posits a more participatory and collaborative model of regulation in which multiple stakeholders, including, depending on the context, government, civil society, business and nonprofit organizations, collaborate to achieve a common purpose. In order to encourage flexibility and innovation, "new governance" approaches favor more process-oriented political strategies like disclosure requirements, benchmarking, and standard-setting, audited self-regulation, and the*

---

[398] Mossialos et al., *Health Systems Governance*, 34.
[399] Ibid.
[400] Katherine Fierlbeck, "The changing contours of experimental governance in European health care", *Social Science & Medicine* 108 (May 2014): 90, https://doi.org/10.1016/j.socscimed.2014.02.040.

> *threat of imposition of default "regulatory regimes" to be applied where there is a lack of good-faith effort at achieving desired goals*[401].

Thus, summing up, the soft law instruments have proven to be quite effective and well tolerated because they provide more productive policy solutions than the formal and rigid forms of legal harmonisation, but also because, by establishing a normative perspective which unifies a huge number of actors and by accepting a common process, they can be used to challenge the dominant ideological force of market-based principles, which can be harmful in healthcare matters[402].

It is also important to underline that the various European instruments of governance are necessary means for the Union in order to fulfil the obligation set out by Article 168(2) TFEU to encourage coordination between Member States in their policies to achieve public health goals and, in particular, to improve the complementarity of their health services in cross-border areas. Moreover, among its roles at EU level, the European Commission may:

> *(...) take any useful initiative to promote such coordination, in particular initiatives aiming at the establishment of guidelines and indicators, the organisation of exchange of best practice, and the preparation of the necessary elements for periodic monitoring and evaluation*[403].

Thus, it is precisely in this context that the numerous new governance mechanisms are created, with the final goal of bringing together, on a voluntary basis, the various and different national health policies.

Soft law instruments can have a "pre-law" function providing preparatory information, such as green papers, action programmes and communications. They can also perform a "post-law" function through interpretative and decisional tools that, even if not mandatory (such as clinical trials standards), constitute a useful source for guidance on the right application of EU law. Finally, softer instruments can also fulfil policy coordination with, for instance, formal mechanisms for a

---

[401] Alana Klein, "Judging as Nudging: New Governance Approaches for the Enforcement of Constitutional Social and Economic Rights", *Columbia Human Rights Law Review* 38, no. 2 (Spring 2008): 351-422.
[402] Fierlbeck, "Changing contours", 89.
[403] TFEU, Article 168(2).

comparison of national systems against benchmarks and for disseminating good practices and codes of conduct[404].

Moreover, the creation of supranational agencies is one of the greatest examples of governance architecture. The agencies, acting independently of the Commission, increasingly became more welcomed by Member States because they work without interfering directly in national affairs and, at the same time, do not expand the Commission's powers. Indeed, despite none of the European Union agencies being independent regulators, they are able to fulfil their respective governance roles, such as the development of standards, the collection of information, and the implementation of specialised programmes outside the Commission's bureaucracy and influence[405].

In particular, we have already seen the importance of the independent agencies in the pharmaceutical sector with the essential role of the EMA in shaping, controlling and ensuring a high level of health protection within the Union. Furthermore, the assignation of the risk assessment function to the EU scientific committee symbolised an attempt to depoliticise healthcare protection and foster credibility in the European scientific decision-making process[406].

Let us now take a quick look at the most used soft law tools in healthcare at the European Union level, what their tasks are, the reasons for their creation, the ways in which they operate and the grounds for their possible termination.

The Open Method of Coordination (OMC) is the most famous soft law mechanism. When it was created in 1997, the OMC was intended to assist the progress of the European Employment Strategy, but, very quickly, its range of action expanded to other policy areas, up to and including healthcare in 2004.

This type of governance has proven to be a useful instrument for the promotion of comparative evaluations of Member States' performances based on the voluntary sharing of best practices and general information[407]. Indeed, each Member State established national reports, based on common indicators, in order to outline and share both the internal current situation

---

[404] Scott L. Greer, "Choosing Paths in European Union Health Policy: A Political Analysis of a Critical Juncture", *Journal of European Social Policy* 18, no. 3 (August 2008): 219-231.

[405] Mossialos et al., *Health Systems Governance*, 36.

[406] Ibid.

[407] Scharpf, *European Social Model*, 645-670.

of the policy area concerned and the best strategies necessary for achieving the more general European goals. The final aim is to monitor and assess the specific national results. Formally, the European Commission only has a monitoring role, but, in practice, the OMC is an efficient means for the establishment of the policy agenda and a further instrument used by the Commission in order to persuade reluctant Member States to implement agreed policies.

In relation to healthcare policy, the outcomes of national evaluations were generally quite mixed because most countries were more likely to report existing policies than develop new ones[408]. The various new EU countries benefited the most from the explanation of other states' best practices and the access to EC expertise that they did not possess. At the same time, the older and more powerful Member States learned a lot from the smaller states because, due to their limited financial resources, they were able to offer more creative and realistic solutions to specific policy problems[409].

What is important to note is that, although it lacks formal sanction capabilities, the effectiveness of the OMC relies on peer pressure and "naming and shaming" tactics, so Member States are encouraged to achieve better and better results rather than see their name among the list of the worst EU countries in a given policy area[410].

Currently, the OMC is not explicitly included in Europe 2020 (the EU's current long-term planning strategy) because it was considered too broad and too unfocused to achieve immediate and quantifiable results. Indeed, in the field of health policy, the use of OMCs has quietly been eclipsed by the use of Joint Action strategies and Reference Networks.

In general, Joint Actions are the funding instrument of the EU Health Programme, which outlines the strategies to protect and ensure a safer and better healthcare in the Union. Two previous Health Programmes have already been conducted and concluded, the first from 2003 to 2007 and the second from 2008 to 2013, which proved to be a successful means to generate knowledge, and exchange best practices and evidence between its members. It is now the time of the Third Health Programme, based on

---

[408] Sandra Kröger, *Five Years Down the Road: an Evaluation of the Streamlining of the OMC in Social Policy Fields* (Brussels: OSE, Briefing paper n. 8, September 2011).

[409] Fierlbeck, "Changing contours", 89-96.

[410] Mossialos et al., *Health Systems Governance*, 35-41.

Regulation (EU) 282/2014[411], which will be operational in the years 2014-2020. The Third Health Programme has the objectives of fostering health and preventing disease by encouraging cooperation between Member States, taking into account the "health in all policies" principle; supporting and complementing Member States' health initiatives; improving patient access to high quality healthcare; protecting EU citizens from cross-border health threats; and contributing to an innovative, efficient and sustainable health system. The Programme is translated into annual work programmes, defining actions in precise priority areas.

Joint Actions, like the OMC, are a collaborative, voluntary, and non-binding exercise in mutual learning with a distinctly limited funding period (up to 36 months). But, unlike the OMC, Joint Actions are clearly detailed policy initiatives funded jointly by the European Commission, Member States and important NGOs, with the aim of defining common priorities and facilitating communication and coordination among Member States by implementing and harmonising existing knowledge rather than producing new ideas. The main strategy is to see whether the EU's money is "well spent". The results are quite concrete and are expected to be permanently institutionalised[412].

A much more recent addition to governance instruments in European healthcare is the European Reference Networks (ERNs). Like Joint Actions, Reference Networks are very specific, and seek to coordinate and integrate existing practices and institutions on a voluntary basis. The framework for this coordination is the Patients Right Directive, which requires the European Commission to work together with Member States to establish networks of excellence within the Union in areas where "critical mass" becomes important in the treatment of particular conditions, as in the case of rare diseases. Indeed, reference networks are established between centres of expertise, laboratories, health professionals and health providers as a useful means to improve access to expertise and innovative practices and foster the exchange of the most recent knowledge across borders. Apart from patient treatment, the networks have other goals such as, for instance, medical training, the establishment of real word registries, and the continuous update of best practices and benchmarks.

---

[411] Regulation (EU) No. 282/2014 of the European Parliament and of the Council of 11 March 2014 on the establishment of a third Programme for the Union's action in the field of health (2014-2020) and repealing Decision No. 1350/2007/EC; 2014 O.J. (L 86) 1, http://data.europa.eu/eli/reg/2014/282/oj.

[412] Fierlbeck, "Changing contours".

Interestingly, what the Directive illustrates is that the execution of hard law in healthcare at the European level does not preclude the use of soft governance techniques but seems, rather, to require them[413].

Another important instrument of governance in the medicinal products sector was the High Level Group on Innovation and Provision of Medicines – the G10 Medicines Group, a small high level group created in 2001 by the European Commission and composed of 13 representatives from Member States, industry and patients entrusted with the task of advising the Commission on ways to increase the competitiveness of the European-based industry in line with public health objectives. In September 2006, the G10 was replaced by a "high level political platform", called the Pharmaceutical Forum, with the aim of discussing and finding mechanisms to enhance information on medicines to patients, improve value for money and access to drugs and ensure quicker access to effective pharmaceuticals, especially in areas partially governed by national laws. Particular attention was devoted to the different national systems of pricing and reimbursement of medicines, which, precisely because of these differences, caused an inequality of access to pharmaceuticals for EU patients. The Forum met two more times, once in 2007 and once in 2008.

The last relevant European soft law mechanism that should be remembered here is the EU HTA network. The Patients' Rights Directive stipulates that the Union shall support and facilitate cooperation between national authorities or bodies responsible for health technology assessment (HTA) designated by the Member States[414]. Briefly and for the sake of clarity, HTA is a multidisciplinary process that reviews the medical, economic, organisational, social and ethical issues related to the use of a health technology in a systematic manner in order to help policy makers to formulate health policies that are safe, effective, patient-focused and cost-effective, and to better understand which technology should be reimbursed at national level. The European Union institutions have been trying to foster national cooperation in this field and, for this reason, the Commission, in 2013, set up a voluntary network (EUnetHTA) consisting of national HTA bodies or agencies covering the entire EU territory with the task of providing strategic and political guidelines for scientific and technical cooperation at EU level. This commitment was integrated with

[413] Ibid.
[414] Directive 2011/24/EU, Article 15.

three consecutive joint actions (EUnetHTA Joint Actions). Currently, the HTA Network develops policy implemented by EUnetHTA Joint Action 3, operative from 2016 to 2020, which tries to increase the use and efficiency of joint HTA work at the European level. In any case, we will address this topic in more detail in Chapter Four.

To summarise, soft approaches to governance will continue to thrive because they fulfil two relevant purposes. The first is a more effective way of getting things done. Indeed, governance instruments facilitate policy development better than a strict imposition of legal harmonisation. This is especially true in the field of healthcare, where rapid technological change, the continuous update of practice guidelines issued by the scientific community, the need for scale economies and interjurisdictional cooperation show that a static traditional system of command-and-control is unable to accommodate a sustainable model of healthcare.

Secondly, soft governance instruments also perform a significant discursive function in the EU, providing an effective vehicle of persuasion for political change. At times, these two functions overlap; at other times, they do not. But there is little reason to believe that they are either irrelevant or destined to disappear[415].

---

415 Fierlbeck, "Changing contours".

PART 2:

ECONOMICS

CHAPTER FOUR

THE REIMBURSEMENT AND PRICING OF PHARMACEUTICALS

4.1 The Overview

In the first part, we saw in detail how the European legislator has tried to harmonise certain aspects of the pharmaceuticals' lifecycle, issuing a series of directives and regulations that, from 1965 to date, outline, together with the remaining national legislation, the current European regulatory system of medicinal products. Indeed, recalling the provision laid down in Article 168(4)(c) TFEU, the European Parliament and the Council can adopt measures setting high standards of quality and safety for medicinal products in order to meet common safety concerns and, in particular, a high level of human health protection, especially where domestic standards would otherwise prevent their achievement. In this way, some issues related to medicines, such as aspects of the marketing authorisation, clinical trials, manufacturing, packaging, labelling, advertising, distribution and pharmacovigilance have been harmonised and have uniform safety, quality and efficacy standards across Member States.

Moreover, we saw that, despite the explicit but extremely limited legal basis, the European legislator has relied on different institutions and competences, especially those in the context of the single market program, in order to extend its influence in the healthcare matter, creating in this way a "patchwork" of regulations.

In this complex situation, a primary role in shaping, clarifying and stimulating the legislator to improve and further develop the regulatory landscape was carried out by the CJEU, which, through its judgments, set policy directions especially on the basis of atypical cases within the single market principle of the free movement of goods and, to some extent, undistorted competition. Finally, to complete the framework of this regulatory patchwork of drugs, are the various soft law instruments that, through a prevalent voluntary adherence system, help Member States to coordinate their policies and learn from each other with regard to the best practices to be implemented in achieving health policy objectives.

However, according to Article 168(7), the responsibilities for the definition of health policies, organisation, delivery and management of health services and medical care and the allocation of the resources assigned to them remain the competence of each Member State. In particular, there are two key features which remain primarily national competences: the pricing and reimbursement of medicinal products.

Indeed, it has been stressed many times that it is fully the Member States' competence to decide which medicines are reimbursed and at what price, and that any voluntary cooperation on pricing and reimbursement between EU countries should remain Member State-driven[416]. As a result, there are many national health schemes within each European country and the pricing and reimbursement of pharmaceuticals are subject to very different rules across the Union. Each Member State uses a different system, adapted to its own economic and health needs, even if everyone faces the common challenge of balancing three overarching objectives: the optimal use of financial resources to ensure the sustainability of healthcare for an ageing European population, access to medicines for EU patients and obtaining rewards for valuable innovation[417].

Furthermore, we saw in the development of EU legislation on medicinal products that only a minimal level of harmonisation has been achieved with respect to pricing with the adoption of the Transparency Directive in 1989. This legislative text imposes a series of procedural requirements designed to verify that national pricing and reimbursement decisions are based on objective and verifiable criteria in order to avoid the creation of possible obstacles to the EU pharmaceutical trade. But, because of the subsequent failure in the achievement of its objective and the repeated infringements of its procedural requirements by Member States, the Directive did not achieve its purpose. For this reason, the Commission proposed a new Transparency Directive in 2012 with a view to simplifying and increasing the respect of such legislation while retaining the original unchanged aims. Nevertheless, such a reforming

---

[416] Council of the European Union, *Council conclusions on strengthening the balance in the pharmaceutical systems in the European Union and its Member States*, 2016 O.J. (C 296) 31, para 6, https://publications.europa.eu/en/publication-detail/-/publication/b49097b2-5096-11e6-89bd-01aa75ed71a1/language-en.

[417] Aysegul Timur and Gabriel Picone, "Regulating The Pharmaceutical Industry in The European Union: A Dilemma Of Achieving A Single Market", *International Business & Economics Research Journal* 8, no. 7 (December 2010): 29-42.

attempt met strong resistance and the proposal was formally withdrawn in 2015.

The different national pharmaceutical pricing and reimbursement regulations create a dilemma to achieve a single market of pharmaceuticals in the Union. Since the beginning of the first communitarian directives related to medicinal products, the Commission has tried to create this single market in order to make the European Union the pharmaceutical industry's natural home. It has been repeatedly argued[418] that the single market would enable the ultimate goal of making authorised medicines accessible to all patients in a fast, safe and sustainable manner. Part of the process is to ensure the strengthening of confidence in the system and to create a competitive market, thus increasing the availability of medicines at lower costs and making the Union able to attract more investment in R&D.

Not only the Commission but also the stakeholders of the pharmaceutical sector are worried about the market fragmentation linked to disparities in national pricing and reimbursement schemes, which create important inequalities between patients in access to medicines and hamper the potential growth of the EU industry.

Indeed, the legal uncertainty that has arisen for the different European national systems and the unnecessary regulatory burdens due to the divergences in the implementation of the Union's legislation has implied a shift of economic and research activity towards the US, especially during the last decade. Additionally, Europe is now facing increasing competition because the geographical balance of the pharmaceutical market is likely to shift gradually towards emerging economies such as China and Brazil.

Thus, losing ground in pharmaceutical innovation is one of the major concerns of European institutions, especially because the pharmaceutical industry is a high technology sector with a high value added per person employed correlation and a high ratio of R&D investment to net sales.

For these reasons, European institutions have been trying to trigger a process in order to make further progress towards a single and sustainable market of pharmaceuticals.

It is also important to note that the achievement of a single market of medicines is further complicated not only by the conflicting interests

[418] See, for example, European Commission, *Communication from the Commission to the European Parliament, the Council, the European Economic and Social Committee and the Committee of the Regions on Safe, Innovative and Accessible Medicines: A Renewed Vision for the Pharmaceutical Sector*, COM (2008) 666 final, https://eur-lex.europa.eu/legal-content/EN/TXT/?uri=COM:2008:0666:FIN.

involved, but also by the unique nature of the research-based industry. Indeed, the functions of demand are divided between patients, prescribing doctors, different characteristics of healthcare systems and the consumers' expectations about the affordable prices of medicines. Notwithstanding the continuous requests expressed by the industry to the Commission asking for certain forms of national price regulation to be removed, the industry cannot be wholly protected from the inter-brand competition from generics following patent expiration or intra-brand competition created by the parallel importing of products from EU countries with lower prices.

The Council and some Member States stressed the fact that the entire system may be imbalanced and that it may not always promote the best possible outcome for patients and society[419].

In particular, in the next section we will focus on the inequalities in access to medicines, especially new health technologies, that patients from smaller EU countries with limited financial resources are forced to suffer because of the different national drug reimbursement systems across the Union. For instance, it often happens that a citizen from a middle-income Member State does not see a specific medicinal product reimbursed by the national system, while another citizen from another Member State does. It is quite obvious that such a system creates major inequalities and discriminations between EU citizens.

The reasons for this problem can be of a double nature. The first one, the simplest and most immediate, is represented by the limited financial resources of some European countries, which, in the context of cost containment, are unable to reimburse certain drugs.

The second one, on the contrary, is more technical and delicate, and concerns the lack of transparency and/or economic evaluation in the way in which it is decided whether a medicinal product, more or less cost-efficient, will be reimbursed or not. In this sense, the Commission has tried to develop and improve the use of health technology assessments (HTA), which offer effective support to national authorities to strike a balance between containing pharmaceutical expenditure and ensuring a fair reward for valuable innovation and access to the best available medicines[420].

Finally, in the last part, we will analyse some of the different techniques used by the national regulators to establish the price of

---

[419] Council of the European Union, *Conclusions,* para 21.
[420] Timur and Picone, "Regulating".

medicines, the mechanisms of cost containment applied to control public expenditure on pharmaceuticals and the economic implications of the different prices set by Member States for the Community trade. These are important aspects to be considered because the prices of pharmaceuticals are a key issue for healthcare, as medicines represent one of the most important cost components in Member States' healthcare budgets. Moreover, the costs are rising faster than Member States' GDP, mainly due to ageing populations and the increasing cost of developing new pharmaceutical technologies. At the same time, the regulation of pharmaceuticals' prices will affect an industrial sector that is a major component of Europe's economy in terms of employment, manufacturing, and R&D[421].

4.2 Member States' Budgets Constraints and Inequalities in Patient Access

We have already seen that the competence of organising and financing healthcare systems remains the prerogative of Member States. The relative differences of the arrangements regard the "basket of care", meaning by whom, how, why and which treatments are covered and provided by national health systems.

The literature usually tends to distinguish between two types of funding systems for health services: on the one hand, the so-called Bismarck systems that are predominantly insurance based and, on the other hand, the tax-based Beveridge systems.

In the first social insurance model, healthcare is predominantly paid for by compulsory health insurance schemes and medical saving accounts. On the contrary, in the Beveridge model, health services, usually public, are organised by government schemes and are thus financed by state taxation in such a way as to cover every citizen[422].

None of the individual health system conforms directly to either the Bismarck or Beveridge models and, usually, in many Member States the two models coexist together with other financing aspects (voluntary health insurance schemes, financing schemes of non-profit institutions serving households, etc.).

Notwithstanding the above-mentioned differences in the organisation of health systems, all Member States face similar problems: the need for

---

[421] Ibid.

[422] Hervey and McHale, *European Union Health Law,* 219-222.

cost containments and concerns about access to patients in the face of the ageing of the population, technological developments and rising expectations[423]. Moreover, universal access to quality healthcare at affordable costs is one of the common values in EU health systems. However, what is really important to note is that about 75% of healthcare expenditure in EU countries is not paid out of pocket by individual citizens, but by third-party payers that are funded by taxes, privately or social health insurance[424]. To be more precise, in the Bismarck systems, regulators (the state) and third-party payers (social insurance) are separated, whereas, in the Beveridge model, the third-party payer is the state that both regulates and funds the system. It is therefore important for third-party payers to establish the process to determine whether, how and how much health technologies should be funded.

The broad principle of universal access to safe, effective and quality healthcare obviously also concerns pharmaceuticals, especially because medicines represent the third most important cost component in Member States' healthcare budgets (following hospital and ambulatory care spending)[425].

Furthermore, despite national differences in the organisation and delivery of healthcare, pharmaceutical funding and coverage[426] issues across the Union are largely common and, in particular, related to achieving efficiency in resource allocation and obtaining value for money.

It has been repeatedly stressed[427] that the different Member States' approaches regarding pharmaceutical prices and reimbursement may lead to disparities in pricing, time-to-market delays and inequalities in the

---

[423] Guy and Sauter, "History", 4.

[424] Source: OECD Health Data 2016.

[425] European Parliament, Directorate-General for Internal Policies, *Differences in Cost of and Access to pharmaceutical products in the EU*, Brussels, March 2011, 16,
http://www.europarl.europa.eu/RegData/etudes/etudes/join/2011/451481/IPOL-ENVI_ET(2011)451481_EN.pdf.

[426] "Coverage" is the process for determining which medical services will be provided, paid for or reimbursed in a specific national health system.

[427] See, for example, Department of Health, *The Pharmaceutical Price Regulation Scheme: Eleventh Report to Parliament*, February 2012,
https://www.gov.uk/government/uploads/system/uploads/attachment_data/file/215156/dh_132793.pdf.

access to medicines in terms of both availability and affordability[428]. The individual affordability of a medicine depends on the extent to which a drug is covered by the health insurer, combined with the cost-sharing burden placed on the patient. The main concern is that high prices of specific pharmaceuticals pose a significant affordability problem to several national health insurance systems, consequently exposing patients to unaffordable co-payments. Reimbursement decisions at the national level determine the coverage of pharmaceuticals, including the level of co-payments to be borne by the patients. Due to the scarcity of financial resources assigned to healthcare, limited budgets, the increasing cost of new health technologies and consumers' expectations, national governments have recognised that not all new medicines can be reimbursed. For this reason, a series of regulatory mechanisms for determining which pharmaceuticals are reimbursed and at what price were introduced. As a result, some pharmaceuticals may not be reimbursed, whereas others are only partially reimbursed[429]. The problem is that national authorities usually base their reimbursement decisions mostly on their budgetary constraints, rather than on the effectiveness of innovative medicines.

Thus, the most obvious cause of such inequalities of access to medicines is the insufficient public financial coverage of the weaker Member States, unable to meet the high costs of new health technologies and to reimburse some specific type of medicines to their own citizens.

Therefore, it is common to see how a citizen of a middle-income EU country (such as Romania or Greece) does not have access to certain medicines, even life-saving ones (as often happens with anticancer pharmaceuticals), because, due to their high cost, he cannot afford to pay for them out of pocket or even see them reimbursed by the national health service. This is a basic need that another citizen, from another Member State, sees, on the contrary, fulfilled.

Indeed, it is quite obvious that pharmaceutical expenditure is associated with per capita GDP levels as well as total health expenditure and is influenced by demographics and domestic policy priorities[430].

This is the reason why inequalities in patient access to pharmaceuticals have further increased after the 2008 financial crisis and the consequent

---

428 European Parliament, Directorate General For Internal Policies, *EU Options for Improving Access to Medicines*, Workshop, Brussels, July 14, 2016. http://www.europarl.europa.eu/RegData/etudes/STUD/2016/587304/IPOL_STU(2016)587304_EN.pdf.

429 European Parliament, *EU Options*, 42.

430 Ibid.

policies to cut public spending[431], which resulted in the healthcare spending collapse. Since that moment, patient access to pharmaceuticals, and to healthcare in general, has been increasingly considered against a background of financial sustainability.

From the statistics of Eurostat and the research of the Directorate-General for Internal Policies[432], two relevant data emerged: first, prices of pharmaceuticals are proportionally higher in Member States with higher levels of per capita income; second, richer Member States spend more on pharmaceuticals. It was also noted that these two facts might be due to higher per capita consumption in volume terms (and obviously higher average pharmaceutical prices too). Manufacturers, for their part, in order to increase their profits, are much more likely to launch and market their medicines in Member States with a high level of reimbursement and comprehensive coverage, given the higher demand. Moreover, since it is recurrent practice for national competent authorities to base their price and reimbursement levels on those of other Member States (through the reference price), it is advantageous for pharmaceutical companies to start marketing their products in a country that can afford the highest price or reimbursement level.

It is therefore evident that the wealthier Member States are in a better position to ensure patient access to the most innovative and expensive medicinal products.

By contrast, weaker EU countries, especially those with lower per capita GDP, are often unable to bear high reimbursement levels or extensive coverage and will therefore have a smaller market due to being unable to attract the largest and most competitive producers. And this is precisely the reason why about two thirds of the pharmaceutical market in the European Union is held by the five largest markets (Germany, UK, France, Italy, and Spain)[433].

Middle-income Member States' limited access is not only the result of different national reimbursement policies, lower income and market size, but it is also influenced by the historical context and national language on the demand-side (for example, the additional costs of the translation of the

---

431 Marina Karanikolos et al., "Financial crisis austerity, and health in Europe", *The Lancet* 381, no. 9874 (April 13): 1323-1331, https://doi.org/10.1016/S0140-6736(13)60102-6.

432 European Parliament, *EU Options*.

433 Ibid.

labelling can be a deterrent for the industry to apply for, or renew, their market authorisation).

Furthermore, it is important to remember that overall patient access and the affordability of pharmaceuticals are also affected by the availability of cheap generic alternatives to expensive branded drugs. Their availability is influenced, in addition to the natural competition constraints, by the original producers' strategies applied to inhibit or delay the penetration of generics into the market.

The importance of ensuring patient access to medicines for all citizens in the Union was addressed by a series of EU initiatives. For instance, in 2008, the European Commission adopted a Communication aiming to, *inter alia*, launch reflections on ways to improve market access[434]. Between 2010 and 2013, the Commission initiated a "Platform on Access to Medicines in Europe" in order to find common soft law approaches to timely and equitable access to medicines in Europe after their marketing authorisation[435]. Moreover, the Commission created the Expert Group on Safe and Timely Access to Medicines for Patients (STAMP), which exchanges information about the experiences of Member States and identifies more effective ways to use the existing EU regulatory tools to improve patient access[436].

More recently, in 2016, the Group of the Progressive Alliance of Socialists and Democrats (S&D) of the European Parliament adopted recommendations aiming to reduce inequalities in access to medicines in the EU[437], which especially grew in the wake of the economic crisis.

---

[434] European Commission, *Communication from the Commission to the European Parliament, the Council, the European Economic and Social Committee and the Committee of the Regions: Safe, Innovative and Accessible Medicines: A Renewed Vision for the Pharmaceutical Sector*, COM (2008) 666 final, http://eurlex.europa.eu/LexUriServ/LexUriServ.do?uri=COM:2008:0666:FIN:en:PDF.

[435] "Corporate responsibility in the pharmaceutical industry", European Commission, last updated October 28, 2018, http://ec.europa.eu/growth/sectors/healthcare/competitiveness/corporate-responsibility/index_en.htm.

[436] "Commission Expert Group on Safe and Timely Access to Medicines for Patients ('STAMP')", European Commission, accessed November 27, 2018, http://ec.europa.eu/health/documents/pharmaceutical-committee/stamp/index_en.htm.

[437] *S&D ENVI Recommendations for better access to medicines in the European Union* (Brussels: S&D position paper, June 7, 2016),

Despite these European initiatives, the regulatory landscape in the Union remains complex and the inequalities in patient access to medicines are still a significant concern. Further research is needed on methods by which market access to medicines may be sped up. Possible areas of benefit include further exploring the use of HTAs.

4.3 Health Technology Assessment

Until now, we have seen that the differences in patient access to medicines within the Union are a consequence of a positive link between Member States' GDP per capita and spending on healthcare per capita and, more generally, the small market size and limited financial resources of modest Member States.

However, this overall vision is limited, since there are other causes that involve the aforementioned inequalities. Indeed, the lack of an adequate approach for an efficient allocation of the scarce resources in a given system is the main one. It is also clear that the simple and unfounded denial of innovative medicines to patients is not an adoptable solution, given the physicians' and patients' contrariety and the absence of the political will to do so. Moreover, measures such as the imposition of price controls or huge price reductions in reimbursements for innovative medicines can have undesired effects on pharmaceuticals' R&D. Thus, given the decreasing public funds and the increasing prices of innovative medicines (notably new treatments for cancer and rare diseases), payers are under pressure to find alternative ways to determine which new health technologies should be reimbursed. In addition, since it is difficult to rapidly increase the scarce resources of a Member State and thus to gather more public funds to be used to cover national health expenditure, it is necessary to find mechanisms that give more value to the scarce financial resources available. In practice, this does not mean getting more money, but giving more value to money.

For these reasons, Member States, in their processes of determining price and reimbursement levels, are increasingly using proper assessments to determine the benefit and the added value of a new health technology. Broadly speaking, there are two main aspects to be considered in the assessment of added value: the scientific analysis of the therapeutic value, linked to the merits of the new medicinal product in comparison to pre-existing alternatives, and the cost effectiveness examination, which is also

---

https://www.socialistsanddemocrats.eu/sites/default/files/position_paper/position_paper_access_to_medecines_en_160607.pdf.

closely connected to the budgetary constraints of a national healthcare system[438]. In general, payers would prefer not to pay for medicines that do not produce any additional benefit compared to the standard of care that is already guaranteed.

The most important form of scientific research used to provide input to policy making in healthcare is certainly the health technology assessment (HTA). Of the various definitions of HTA that can be found in the literature, the most authoritative is the one provided by the International Network of Agencies of HTA (INHTA) which defines the assessment as

> *(...) the systematic evaluation of the properties and effects of a health technology, addressing the direct and intended effects of this technology, as well as its indirect and unintended consequences, and aimed mainly at informing decision making regarding health technologies. HTA is conducted by interdisciplinary groups that use explicit analytical frameworks drawing on a variety of methods*[439].

Since its origins in the 1970s, the HTA has expanded its scope of action not only to innovative medicines but also to medical devices, medical procedures, and organisational systems for care provision, as well as the economic and societal consequences of implementing health technologies[440]. Moreover, from the first moment of the HTA's diffusion in Europe, new agencies, institutions, organisational and academic units, and governmental and non-governmental bodies were created in order to dedicate themselves to the evaluation of health technologies. HTA is therefore a multidisciplinary activity designed to support the decision-making process at policy level, especially regarding resource allocation and availability, the reimbursement and price of medicines, the range of coverage, and issuing guidance on the use of health technologies.

For this reason, the HTA has been metaphorised as a bridge between the world of research and the world of decision-making[441]. Indeed,

---

438 European Commission, *Pharmaceutical Sector Inquiry*, 492-494.

439 "What is Health Technology Assessment (HTA)?", The International Network of Agencies for Health Technology Assessment, accessed February 5, 2019, http://www.inahta.org/.

440 Marcial Velasco-Garrido and Reinhard Busse, "Health Technology Assessment: An introduction to objectives, role of evidence, and structure in Europe" (Policy Brief, European Observatory on Health Systems and Policies, 2005).

441 Renaldo N. Battista, "Towards a paradigm for technology assessment", in *The scientific basis of health services,* eds. Michael Peckham and Richard Smith (London: BMJ Publishing Group, 1996), 11-18.

medicines' evidence-based principles are transferred, through this bridge, to healthcare policy and management in order to build a body of best practices and to provide the best available evidence contributing to the sustainability and accessibility of national health systems. The HTA process can be applied to take different types of decisions at different levels of the health system. Therefore, the necessary information can vary based on the different actors involved (managers, authorities, politicians, hospitals, etc.), the specific technology to be assessed, the methodology to be used, and the extent of the assessment. Once the policy question of the assessment to be conducted has been defined, the HTA protocol has been elaborated and all the relevant information has been collected (possibly after having re-contacted the commissioner), it is time to define the policy question in terms of safety; its efficacy and effectiveness; psychologically, socially and ethically; organisationally and professionally; and economically. It is logical to start the assessment with the safety aspect and then proceed in order with the other sequential ones given that their analysis might not be necessary if the previous ones have already provided a negative answer. Once the assessment is completed, a final HTA report will be drafted, published and discussed[442].

The importance of HTA has grown significantly in the last few decades, especially due to the reductions of public funds designated to the healthcare sector. Nowadays, the HTA is a globally recognised process, used in almost all European countries, aiming to maximise the social value of health technologies while ensuring, at the same time, that they are rewarding in terms of consumed resources[443]. Moreover, the relationship between HTAs and coverage decisions was analysed and globally discussed by the Health Technology Assessment International (HTAi) Policy Forum at a meeting held in 2011 in the United Kingdom. The interaction between the HTA and coverage decisions was thought about in terms of improving: patient access to appropriate interventions; the evidence base and transparency for coverage decisions; and the efficiency of the development of new products. Indeed, the coordination between these functions could reduce the overall burden of evidence requirements,

---

[442] Reinhard Busse et al., "Best Practice in undertaking and reporting health technology assessments: Working Group 4 Report", *International Journal of Technology Assessment in Health Care* 18, no. 2 (April 2002): 361-422.

[443] Oriana Ciani, Rosanna Tarricone, Aleksandra Torbica, "Diffusion and use of health technology assessment in policy making: What lessons for decentralised healthcare systems?", *Health Policy* 108, no. 2-3 (December 2012): 194-202, https://doi.org/10.1016/j.healthpol.2012.09.017.

speeding up, in this way, patient access to new pharmaceuticals and decreasing unnecessary barriers to innovation[444].

In the last twenty years, the majority of Member States have started to introduce HTA systems at a national or regional level. Hence, within the Union, there are, on one side, countries with a relatively long tradition in the use of HTAs with specialised and institutionalised agencies, and, on the other side, countries that are only at an early stage or that have dedicated only limited resources to carry out this assessment. Greece, for example, has only recently introduced the HTA as a means to determine the coverage level in light of the country's financial constraints and has decided to reimburse only medicines which have already been affirmatively evaluated in other countries[445].

From recent research conducted by the EUnetHTA, it has emerged that the HTA is frequently part of a larger formal procedure to inform reimbursement decisions (97% and 91% for pharmaceutical and non-pharmaceutical health technologies respectively) and pharmaceutical pricing decisions (69%)[446]. In addition, Member States have set out governance procedures which specify the details for the inclusion of the HTA in their formal decision-making process and support the accuracy and accountability of the procedure.

Generally speaking, bodies across the Union responsible for conducting HTAs can be of a double nature: on the one hand, there are independent review entities that develop and diffuse assessment reports on different topics, and, on the other hand, there are organisms with governmental mandates (national or regional), typically with the main task of helping with decisions in relation to the pricing and reimbursement of health technologies[447]. Usually, HTA organisations are not regulatory

444 Chris Henshall et al., "Interactions between health technology assessment, coverage, and regulatory processes: Emerging issues, goals, and opportunities", *International Journal of Technology Assessment in Health care* 27, no. 3 (July 2011): 253-260, https://doi.org/10.1017/S0266462311000262.

445 Sotiris Vandoros and Tom Stargardt, "Reforms in the Greek pharmaceutical market during the financial crisis", *Health Policy* 109, no. 1 (January 2013): 1-6, https://doi.org/10.1016/j.healthpol.2012.08.016.

446 EUnetHTA, *An analysis of HTA and reimbursement procedures in EUnetHTA partner countries: final report*, EUnetHTA WP7 research and analysis activity 1, 2017.

447 Corinna Sorenson, Michael Drummond and Panos Kanavos, *Ensuring value for money in health care: the role of health technology assessment in the European Union*, (Copenhagen: European Observatory on Health Systems and Policies, 2008).

bodies and thus do not hold decision-making powers, however they can be considered quite similar to political institutions because they are often public bodies financed by taxes and have the institutional aim of improving the healthcare system[448]. This heterogeneity of HTA institutions is a direct consequence of the variety of traditions, history and socioeconomic contexts of healthcare systems within the Union[449].

Differences between Member States not only exist in the types of entity responsible for conducting the assessment level, but also and especially at the resulting recommendations level. These substantial variations across EU countries can have a negative impact on the affordability of and patient access to innovative medicines and can be the direct consequence of the different capacity and availability of existing relevant structures responsible for conducting HTAs, the function and content of HTAs, and the approaches used for their assessment and evaluation[450]. In particular, the reasons for HTA outcomes can vary because of the several selection criteria of the medicines used by the agencies for which an HTA is conducted, the different economic models and comparators for the same drug, the duration of HTA processes (i.e. 32 to 56 weeks in the UK versus 17 to 18 weeks in Sweden), the amount of evidence available, and the level of transparency. The methodologies used to conduct HTAs differ from country to country and also between regions when decision-making is decentralised (such as, for example, in Italy and Spain).

Moreover, the situation is further complicated because of the diverging interpretation of the same evidence and the different views on what is considered to be the "added-value" of an innovative medicine. Indeed, all Member States contemplate clinical/therapeutic progress, but only some of them also look at benefits to the quality of life. In addition, only a small number of Member States take into consideration the broader economic benefits of new pharmaceuticals, such as, for example, the cost savings of informal care[451]. The effective implementation of HTA recommendations also appears to depend upon the role of the HTA agency (i.e. binding or non-binding recommendations) and at which level the entity operates

---

[448] Camilla P. Nielsen et al., "Involving stakeholders and developing a policy for stakeholder involvement in the European network for health technology assessment, EUnetHTA", *International Journal of Technology Assessment in Health Care* 25, no. S2 (December 2009): 84-91, https://doi.org/10.1017/S0266462309990729.

[449] Velasco-Garrido and Busse, "Health Technology Assessment".

[450] EUnetHTA, *Analysis*.

[451] European Commission, *Pharmaceutical Sector Inquiry,* 492-494.

(national, regional or local/hospital)[452]. In addition, the involvement of stakeholders, who can provide information, technical support and expertise to HTA bodies, has also been shown to be limited, with potentially negative impacts on HTA recommendations[453], especially because such involvement could also guarantee the legitimacy of the final assessment and prevent conflict after the technologies have entered the market[454].

Finally, governments can make different reimbursement decisions on the basis of the outcome resulting from the same assessment if there is a difference in the perceptions of the value of the available data[455].

All of these divergences reflect the multiplicity of cultures, traditions, and general organisational structures of national healthcare systems[456].

The result is the absence of uniform HTA standards and requirements generally accepted throughout the Union, increasing, consequently, the costs and complexity of bringing innovation to the internal market, which is also because pharmaceutical companies have to prepare submission files for different jurisdictions with different comparators in individual European countries.

In conclusion, given these differences and their relative negative consequences in patient access and development of new medicines, there is a need to develop broadly acceptable HTA mechanisms and a more consistent and sustainable HTA approach within the Union. In order to achieve such goals, it is necessary to foster cooperation between the numerous national HTA bodies, third-party payers and pharmaceutical producers.

For this reason, different initiatives have been implemented by the Commission to harmonise or standardise the HTA processes, to foster

---

452 European Parliament, *Differences*.

453 Marianna Cavazza and Claudio Jommi, "Stakeholders involvement by HTA Organisations: Why is so different?", *Health Policy* 105, no. 2-3 (May 2012): 236-245, https://doi.org/10.1016/j.healthpol.2012.01.012.

454 Julia Abelson et al., "Bringing 'the public' into health technology assessment and coverage public decisions: From principles to practice", *Health Policy* 82, no. 1 (June 2007): 37-50, https://doi.org/10.1016/j.healthpol.2006.07.009.

455 Sarah Kleijnen et al., "Relative Effectiveness Assessment of Pharmaceuticals: Similarities and Differences in 29 Jurisdictions", *Value in Health* 15, no. 6 (September – October 2012): 954-960, https://doi.org/10.1016/j.jval.2012.04.010.

456 Ciani, Tarricone and Torbica, "Diffusion". See also, Aleksandra Torbica, Rosanna Tarricone and Michael Drummond, "Does the approach to economic evaluation in health care depend on culture, values, and institutional context?", *The European Journal of Health Economics* 19, no. 6 (July 2018): 769-774, https://doi.org/10.1007/s10198-017-0943-1.

their transparency, quality and comprehensiveness, and facilitate the sharing of information and cross-border expertise. This Commission's continuous support and push for cooperation between national authorities and HTA bodies is also a duty established by Article 15 of the Patient's Rights Directive.

An important and recent initiative is the establishment, in 2006, of the European Network for Health Technology Assessment (EUnetHTA), which has the aim of developing a sustainable European network for HTAs and to create effective tools to transfer information between members who decided to cooperate on a voluntary basis.

The push towards an increasing use of this assessment method and the attempt to create a uniform HTA process will reduce duplications of efforts and improve efficiency in the use of resources.

From 2016 to 2020, the scientific and technical cooperation of the new HTA network by the EUnetHTA will be conducted through the so-called Joint Action 3, which has the aim of increasing the use, quality and efficiency of joint HTA work at a European level. The activity supports Member States in receiving relevant HTA information that is objective, reliable, timely and comparable. And it is precisely in this regard that one of the most important creations of the EUnetHTA stems: the HTA Core Model® (Figure 4-1). This was designed to provide a common format of relevant HTA information to support its sharing between members both at the national and international levels[457]. Indeed, the nine domains of the model are intended to standardise the framework for conducting the assessment[458].

Furthermore, the European Commission, through, *inter alia*, additional projects and stakeholder consultations[459], is continuously trying to foster cooperation in this field. In this regard, on 31 January 2018, the European Commission published a proposal for a new Regulation on HTA[460]. Indeed,

---

[457] Finn Børlum Kristensen, "Development of European HTA: from Vision to EUnetHTA", Michael Quarterly 9 (2012): 147-156.

[458] Nicola Allen et al., "A Comparison of Reimbursement Recommendations by European HTA Agencies: Is There Opportunity for Further Alignment?", *Frontiers in Pharmacology* 8 (June 2017): 384, https://doi.org/10.3389/fphar.2017.00384.

[459] See, for example: European Commission, *Strengthening of the EU cooperation on Health Technology Assessment (HTA)*, 2016, http://ec.europa.eu/smart-regulation/roadmaps/docs/2016_sante_144_health_technology_assessments_en.pdf.

[460] European Commission, *Proposal for a Regulation of the European Parliament and of the Council on health technology assessment and amending Directive 2011/24/EU*, COM (2018) 51 final,
https://ec.europa.eu/health/sites/health/files/technology_assessment/docs/com2018_51_en.pdf.

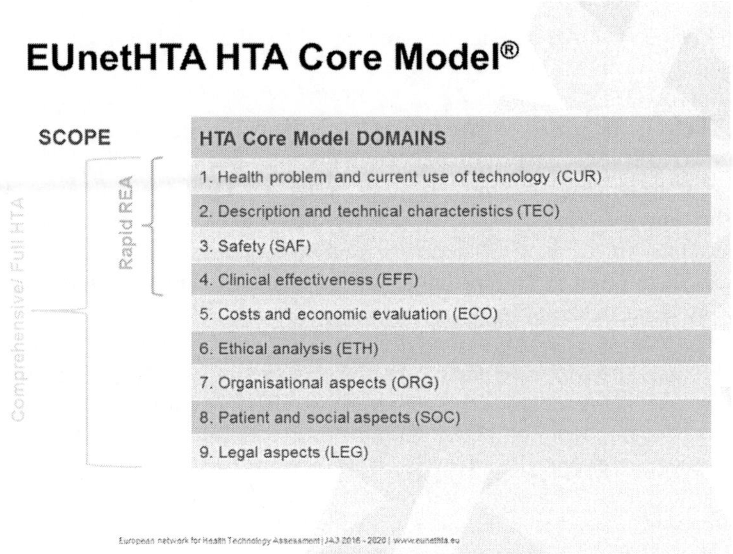

Figure 4-1 EUnetHTA HTA Core Model® Domains[461] (See centrefold for this image in colour)

if the ongoing collaboration (EUnetHTA and its Joint Actions) has demonstrated the benefits of cooperation at EU level, the current model of cooperation has not completely eliminated the fragmentation of the internal market or the duplication of assessments. Without a strong European initiative, long-term HTA cooperation between Member States is unlikely to be strengthened, with the potential risk of losing the results achieved. For this reason, the main goal pursued by the European Commission with this new proposal for a Regulation is the consolidation of international cooperation on HTAs through the identification of common methods to evaluate the added value of health technologies, especially from a clinical point of view, avoiding in this way the duplication of efforts and improving the availability of innovative health technologies for European patients. Indeed, the Commission is convinced that a new set of rules for the joint assessment of new technologies can lay the foundations for permanent cooperation between Member States, gaining, in the long term, economies of scale, a greater predictability of

[461] Source: "HTA Core Model", EUnetHTA, accessed November 28, 2018, https://www.eunethta.eu/hta-core-model/.

the business environment, and increased quality and transparency for patients.

There is a need to ensure that HTAs will be conducted in all Member States with the most uniform methods possible. Therefore, the four principle elements of the proposal are: the implementation of joint evaluations of clinical aspects such as safety and transparency for some products, joint scientific consultations, the identification of emerging health technologies, and voluntary cooperation in HTAs for technologies not included in the proposal. All these activities will be conducted under the direction of a Coordination Group composed of national experts.

Finally, the proposal seems feasible because it shows the intention to standardise HTA methods that are binding only for national HTA agencies and not for national competent authorities that regulate market access, and as such respect the responsibilities of Member States to organise their health services and, most of all, leave the evaluation of economic, social and ethical aspects at the national level. Indeed, the proposal focuses on the clinical HTA domains, which are typically based on global evidence, while non-clinical HTA domains remain Member State-driven given that these are matters that are more sensitive to national contexts.

On 3 October 2018, the European Parliament approved the proposal. In this regard, Soledad Cabezón Ruiz, the MEP in charge of steering the plans through Parliament, specified that

> *(...) at the moment each member state does its own assessment of each new medicine or medical device to assess if it's better than existing products. Not only is this inefficient and duplicates efforts, it also means opportunities to improve the quality of healthcare technology are being missed. These rules will improve healthcare technology so that patients can enjoy better and faster treatment*[462].

In the next step, MEPs will start negotiations for a first-reading agreement with the Council, once the Council has defined its position.

It is expected that, once it has been adopted and entered into force, the Regulation will be applicable after three years. Then, from the date of

---

[462] "Health technologies: 'Opportunities to improve the quality are being missed", European Parliament News, October 4, 2018, http://www.europarl.europa.eu/news/en/headlines/society/20180927STO14537/interview-boosting-eu-cooperation-on-assessment-of-medicine (accessed November 2018).

application, three years will be granted for Member States to adapt to the new system.

4.4 Pharmaceuticals' Pricing: Methods and Implications

As has already been pointed out, Member States have the competence to determine their own national pricing and reimbursement regulation of pharmaceuticals. Indeed, only a minimal level of European harmonisation has been achieved with the Transparency Directive of 1989, which, because of strong resistance from governments, has not been updated and reformed. For this reason, the pharmaceutical pricing and reimbursement systems are very complex and differ from country to country. The Union panorama is characterised by numerous schemes and policies adapted to national needs (such as, *inter alia*, supporting domestic industry, ensuring patient access, and increasing employment), the legal and historical context, economic development, the general level of income, and the organisation of healthcare. Moreover, these policies are regularly reviewed and adjusted to new priorities, patients' demands, and market evolutions.

Nevertheless, despite the differences, it is necessary to remember that the various national systems are connected to the realisation of European policy objectives, especially the internal market, undistorted competition, sustainable R&D, human health protection, and, of course, high standards of quality and safety for medicinal products[463].

In this section we will analyse how the price of each drug is determined at a national level; what measures are taken to contain the ever increasing costs of these products and public health spending; the problems that such market fragmentation entails; and, finally, future trends and possible solutions to be adopted.

Medicines are considered special "merit goods" rather than common "consumer goods"[464]. From the demand side, patients are not typical consumers, especially because they do not directly pay for medicines (out-of-pocket), but also because there are third-party payers, who can mostly afford pharmaceutical expenses. In addition, three decision-making units usually determine demand: patients, prescribers (i.e. physicians) and dispensers (i.e. pharmacists)[465].

---

[463] TFEU, Article 168(4)(c).

[464] OECD Health Policy Studies, *Pharmaceutical Pricing Policies in a Global Market* (Paris: OECD Publishing, 2008).

[465] European Parliament, *Differences*.

Instead, from the supply side, pharmaceutical companies, like any type of industry, attempt to get the highest possible price for their in-patent products, especially during the period of monopoly rent. As a consequence, price competition in this market is hindered even when there are alternatives with similar efficacy.

For these reasons, the pricing of medicines is an example of market failure and therefore does not respond to the normal market rules[466].

Generally speaking, medicines' prices can be determined by following different approaches and criteria as the basis for price setting.

For example, cost-based pricing (CbP), originally used in southern EU countries, involves the price of every single drug being determined by taking into account the major cost items incurred by the pharmaceutical companies (e.g. manufacturing, R&D, marketing) in developing such medicines. But, because of the many difficulties in establishing the single cost items, especially of the biggest industries, this type of scheme is no longer applied within the Union[467].

Moreover, following the cost-plus criteria, a medicine's price might be calculated on the basis of costs, plus a certain profit margin.

Another approach is the value-based price (VbP), which is established on the perceived value that consumers give to the individual drug. This approach should at least determine the price that maximises an individual's willingness to pay[468], using HTA as a measuring instrument.

The most followed approach used to establish a pharmaceutical's price is the reference-based price (RbP). Originally introduced in Germany and currently applied in different forms around the Union, it applies to clusters of competing products in the same relevant market, which basically means that the cost of a pharmaceutical is based on the cost of similar treatments for the same indication. First, it is necessary to set a price cap for a group of substances considered equivalent and grouped in the same therapeutic clusters and then refer to the domestic or foreign prices of the products already on the market[469]. When the price is based on the lowest priced medicine in the group, the reference-based price has proven to be effective

---

[466] Livio Garattini, Alessandro Curto and Nick Freemantle, "Pharmaceutical Price Schemes in Europe: Time for a 'Continental' One?", *PharmacoEconomics* 34, no. 5 (May 2016): 423-426, https://doi.org/10.1007/s40273-015-0377-5.

[467] Ibid.

[468] Michael E. Porter, "What Is Value in Health Care?", *The New England Journal of Medicine* 363, no. 26 (December 23, 2010): 2477-2481, https://doi.org/10.1056/NEJMp1011024.

[469] Garattini, Curto and Freemantle, "Pharmaceutical".

in encouraging health professionals to utilise, on the one hand, more expensive agents in patients with side effects and, on the other hand, the least expensive agents as first-line therapy[470].

The problem is that most Member States are under growing pressures due to ageing populations, expensive new technologies, an inability to entirely fund health expenditures and patients' increasing expectations. The financial crisis of 2008 has further imposed budget constraints on public expenditure on domestic healthcare. Moreover, the Council of the European Union noted with concern that patients' access to effective and affordable medicines is endangered by high and unsustainable prices[471]. High prices are sometimes imposed by pharmaceutical companies, which, thanks to patent and data exclusivity systems granted to them in order to recover their investments in R&D, entail market exclusivity (for up to 11 years) and monopoly power for protected inventions. Indeed, patents protect inventions for a nominal period of 20 years that, with a Supplementary Protection Certificate, can be extended for up to a further five years[472].

The overall situation is further complicated because, in some countries with a decentralised healthcare system (for example, Italy), there can be various domestic prices for the same product, depending on the purchasing procedures and the distribution channels (hospitals and pharmacies)[473].

In response to all these pressures, governments try to negotiate prices with the industry in order to reduce costs and obtain better purchasing conditions by using different types of either cost shifting or cost containment measures or a drive for healthcare efficiency, which can be considered both as challenges or opportunities for industry[474].

Indeed, medicines' prices are very often calculated from the maximum possible price that the market could bear, and this is the reason why it is necessary for authorities to ensure that prices are not more than consumers/patients would be reasonably willing to pay on the grounds of

---

470 Lisa L. Ioannides-Demos, Joseph E. Ibrahim, John J. McNeil, "Reference-Based Pricing Schemes: Effect on Pharmaceutical Expenditure, Resource Utilisation and Health Outcomes", *Pharmacoeconomics* 20, no. 9 (August 2002): 577-591, https://doi.org/10.2165/00019053-200220090-00002.

471 Council of the European Union, *Conclusions,* para 16.

472 European Parliament, *EU Options.*

473 Garattini, Curto and Freemantle, "Pharmaceutical".

474 Nigel Gregson et al., "Pricing Medicines: Theory and Practice, Challenges and Opportunities", *Nature Review Drug Discovery* 4, no. 2 (February 2005): 121-130, https://doi.org/10.1038/nrd1633.

public health, efficiency and social security[475]. National governments and third-party payers in general have implemented many different measures, some with a pure cost focus and others intended to increase efficiency, ranging from controls and incentives to directly influence supply and/or demand or indirectly reduce expenditures. Some measures apply to the initial price when the product is marketed (initial price), while others apply to posterior price changes[476]. Moreover, the level of the distribution chain when the price regulation is implemented may also cause differences between Member States.

Finally, there are fundamental differences between free-pricing systems, where medicines can be priced without restriction at launch, and price-controlled systems, where stakeholders can control the initial price setting. Indeed, free-pricing systems are regulated through profit control[477] or reimbursement regulations through internal reference pricing and/or the use of HTA[478].

Let us now focus on the supply-side measures both in relation to in-patent and off-patent (generics) medicines. Controls of pharmaceutical prices can be done through regulatory schemes (such as direct fixed price controls, profit controls and reference prices) and/or the support of price competition by lowering the market barriers to entry.

Fixed price controls (also referred to as direct price controls) consist of setting fixed maximum prices to medicines that can be reasonably afforded by a specific health system. The measures used for this purpose are of various types and can be: price caps, price/volume tradeoffs, cost-plus pricing, or negotiated prices.

The most criticised method to setting prices, especially because of the lack of transparency, is negotiation. Indeed, some national governments (such as Austria, France, Italy, Portugal, and Spain) negotiate prices directly with the individual pharmaceutical companies, but the criteria used, which are not clear most of the time, leave too much to the authority's discretion. In this regard, the Directorate-General for Internal Policies has stressed that the price agreed during negotiations is usually not unreasonably high or low because, if it is true that producers holding a patent have market power and are monopolists, it is also true that this power is balanced by the fact that public health regulators and third-party

[475] Mossialos, Walley and Mrazek, *Regulating*, 10.
[476] Timur and Picone, "Regulating".
[477] Mossialos, Walley and Mrazek, *Regulating*, 10.
[478] European Parliament, *Differences*, 34.

payers, as single purchasers on behalf of patients, are monopolists too[479]. It may also frequently happen that, through negotiations, prices are fixed based on volume projections (price-volume agreements).

Many Member States use additional instruments to further decrease pharmaceutical expenditures, such as, for instance: mandatory discounts; specific reductions in the final price accorded to some institutional payers; price cuts; freezes; rebates on a specified proportion of sales over a given time period; and payback clauses if the volume agreed is exceeded, obliging producers to return part of their excess revenue to purchasers[480].

In conclusion, it is important to say that direct price controls may slow price increases or induce lower prices. This result is often overshadowed by increases in expenditures caused by growing consumption and the high costs of new innovative health technologies[481].

Profit control (or rate-of-return regulation) is a unique form of indirect price control used to determine in-patent pharmaceutical prices. It is applied only in the UK, a free-pricing system, with the so-called Pharmaceutical Price Regulation Scheme (PPRS). This type of mechanism provides that, through a voluntary agreement between the governmental Department of Health and the branded pharmaceutical industry, companies' profits on sales to the UK National Health Service (NHS) are set below a certain threshold, whilst also allowing pricing flexibility up to that threshold.

The aim of such a mechanism is to ensure that the NHS has access to good quality branded medicines at reasonable prices and, at the same time, to guarantee a fair return for producers and reward innovation. Re-negotiations of the scheme are usually associated with price cuts[482].

Special attention must be paid to reference pricing.

Within the reference pricing methods, we can distinguish internal price referencing, in which prices might also be based on the cost of similar treatments for the same indication in a given health system, and External Reference Pricing (ERP) (also known as international reference pricing),

---

479 Ibid., 36.

480 Jaime Espín and Joan Rovina, *Analysis of differences and commonalities in pricing and reimbursement systems in Europe*, *Final Report* (Brussels: European Commission, June 2007),
https://ec.europa.eu/docsroom/documents/7605?locale=en.

481 Mossialos, Walley and Mrazek, *Regulating*, 10.

482 European Parliament, *Differences*, 37.

which consists, according to the definition of the World Health Organisation (WHO), of

> *(...) the practice of using the price(s) of a medicine in one or several countries in order to derive a benchmark or reference price of the product in a given country*[483].

In this way, changes of the price of a specific medicine charged in one country will influence the relative price in other countries.

Regarding internal reference pricing, first of all, it is important to underline that is it not a pricing system, but a reimbursement one, which sets a common reimbursement level for a group of medicines with the ultimate aim of creating savings for third-party payers. Indeed, it is a system that determines a common reimbursement level for a group of interchangeable and comparable medicines[484]. If a medicine is priced above the reference price, the patient pays the difference plus any other co-payments. This system is also useful for providing patients with a financial incentive to choose cheaper medicinal products (i.e. without co-payments) while at the same time generating cost-containment for healthcare budgets in the short term[485]. Such a system is used by almost every Member State in the European Union as a strategy for containing public healthcare expenditure, while still pushing the pharmaceutical industry to compete with the reference priced products.

By contrast, external reference pricing is the most common criterion used for setting a pharmaceutical's price and almost all Member States have implemented it (except for the UK and Sweden[486]). Only Belgium, Finland, Italy, Poland, Germany and Spain use ERP as supportive information for establishing the price of a new drug.

The main problem is that the ERP systems diverge between EU countries because of the different levels of accuracy, methods of

---

[483] "Glossary", The WHO Collaboration Centre for Pricing and Reimbursement Policies, accessed November 27, 2018, http://whocc.goeg.at/Glossary/PreferredTerms/External%20price%20referencing.

[484] Pieter Dylst, Arnold G. Vulto, Steven Simoens, "Reference pricing systems in Europe: characteristics and consequences", *Generics and Biosimilars Initiative Journal* 1, no. 3-4 (2012): 127-131, https://doi.org/10.5639/gabij.2012.0103-4.028.

[485] Dylst, Vulto and Simoens, "Reference".

[486] Mondher Toumi et al., *External reference pricing of medicinal products: simulation-based considerations for cross-country coordination. Final report*, (Brussels: European Commission, 2014), https://ec.europa.eu/health/sites/health/files/healthcare/docs/erp_reimbursement_medicinal_products_en.pdf.

calculation for computing the price (e.g. average price, lowest price and others), information available, the number of countries included in the basket, and the categories of medicines for which the price is estimated[487].

Although ERP is widely used as a means of cost containment by reducing prices, there are some debates about its potential impact. In particular, concerns have been raised because ERP is an arbitrary measure that targets prices while ignoring specific domestic health priorities. Moreover, it has been underlined that this type of reference price can also cause uncertainty on the industry's innovativeness, especially due to the impact of exchange rate fluctuations on reference prices[488]. Finally, as has already been mentioned in relation to reimbursement, by using the practice of ERP, producers are discouraged from placing their medicinal products on the market of a certain country if that country's price influences third countries, or if it is likely to encourage parallel exports because the price imposed is too low. These practices also have the potential to limit patient access to medicines, and, although the industry tries to control ERP, it has little capacity to influence it[489].

So far, we have discussed the supply-side pricing methods for in-patent pharmaceuticals. It is now time to focus on the supply-side regulation for off-patent pharmaceutical (known generally as generics). In particular, it is important to discuss the two main policies followed by third-party payers: tendering for pharmaceuticals consumed in primary care, and price caps.

Tendering is a common measure for the procurement of medicinal products for hospitals. The lowest price bidder who wins the official tender gains the right to supply the whole market. The body issuing the tender establishes the terms concerning whether a single product can replenish the entire market or whether competitors selling their products at the same tender price also have the same right.

Tendering is a very effective means for the reduction of generics' prices, with the added advantage of not limiting innovation as it regards only medicines with patents that have already been exhausted.

---

487 Cécile Rémuzat et al., "Overview of external reference pricing systems in Europe", *Journal of Market Access & Health Policy* 3, no. 1 (September 2015): 1-11, https://doi.org/10.3402/jmahp.v3.27675.

488 Panos Kanavos and Sotiris Vandoros, "Competition in Prescription Drug Markets: Is Parallel Trade the Answer?", *Managerial and Decision Economics* 31, no. 5 (2010): 325-338,
https://EconPapers.repec.org/RePEc:wly:mgtdec:v:31:y:2010:i:5:p:325-338.

489 Rémuzat et al., "Overview".

However, there are concerns that tendering could restrain competition in the long run, especially because of the exit from the market of generics manufacturers who do not win any tender. With such exits, the level of market concentration would rise, thus leading to a possible increase in the prices of generics, not necessarily back to the level prior to tendering, but part of the price reduction is expected to be deviated[490]. Less competition is not only a fear for governments, but also for the European Commission, among whose main purposes is the maintenance of undistorted competition within the internal market.

Price capping is the practice to set price ceilings on products. First, it mirrors the situation in the original market where maximum prices are established to be applied afterwards to generics once the branded product patent has expired.

In principle, this measure mainly aims to generate savings for healthcare budgets through containing costs by limiting the high prices of medicines, both branded and generics, and encouraging the consumption of generics[491]. The uses of such a practice, the prices linked to originators, and the acceptable price levels differ between countries depending on a range of factors including budget constraints, prescribing practices, and utilisation trends[492].

The measure of fixing prices can provide an alternative to simple cost-based regulation, but it is subject to bias and may not be completely transparent. Nevertheless, the European Commission concludes that those Member States which did not enforce price caps have seen a faster uptake of generics and that, over time, the prices of these medicinal products have decreased to a greater extent[493].

It is also worth briefly discussing the actions used in the various Member States on the demand side, which targets the prescribing physicians', the dispensing pharmacies' and the patients' behaviour.

The demand side of the pharmaceutical market has certain particularities that can cause an inefficient use of resources when purchasing medicines. First, patients rely on physicians to decide which health treatment is best suited to their health situation. Second, patients tend to acquire a higher amount of more expensive drugs (the "moral

490 European Parliament, *Differences*, 39.

491 Kurt R. Brekke, Ingrid Koenigbauer, Odd Rune Straume, "Reference pricing of pharmaceuticals", *Journal of Health Economics* 26, no. 3 (2007): 613-642.

492 Mossialos, Walley and Mrazek, *Regulating*.

493 European Commission, *Pharmaceutical Sector Inquiry*.

hazard"), especially because they do not bear the majority of the costs. Third, cultural issues in the prescription of medicines and in their consumption can deteriorate the moral hazard problem. Fourth, pharmacists may dispense more expensive drugs even if cheaper alternatives exist in order to gain economic advantages. Finally, patients are willing to pay more if they believe that one treatment is better than another[494].

Different regulatory mechanisms are implemented in Member States in order to avoid inefficiencies, educate stakeholders, and influence the behaviours of patients, physicians and pharmacists, and, thus, reduce costs.

Several different policies exist to control prescribing practices: generic prescribing, financial/non-financial incentives, prescription monitoring, and audits, alongside the use of clinical practice guidelines and evidence-based medicines.

For example, in some Member States, the prescription of generics is compulsory in order to minimise the dispensing of branded medicines and reduce costs. Among the financial incentives there are monetary rewards for achieving prescription targets and remaining within prescription limits.

Unfortunately, the influence of such policies in many Member States is limited. In addition, even when they are applied, the evaluation of the results obtained thanks to these measures is constrained by the lack of comprehensive information systems tracking prescriptions[495].

Among the policies directed at patients, cost-sharing measures, the improvement of accessible systems providing adequate information and the encouragement of the use of over-the-counter medicines excel.

Nowadays, the Internet is the main source of information for patients, while an exclusive reliance on medical doctors is weakening in relative terms. For this reason, some national health authorities maintain and regulate some websites providing information on pharmaceuticals and other health matters. Nonetheless, risks of misinformation remain very high.

Cost-payments or out-of-pocket (OOP) payments are set during reimbursement decisions in order to ease the public expenditure burden on health and to reduce the unnecessary moral hazard. However, concerns have been raised about co-payments because they may cause inequalities in patient access if people cannot afford to pay for medicines.

---

494 European Parliament, *Differences*, 45.

495 Ibid., 45-47.

Another economic mechanism is to establish over-the-counter pharmaceuticals (OTC)[496], available without a prescription. In principle, OTC products are reimbursed only if they are listed in positive formularies and are, at the same time, prescribed by physicians. Classifying medicinal products as OTCs is a useful means to shift certain costs from statutory health insurance to the individual; to foster individuals' responsibility in self-treatment; and to extend a product's life when it is nearing its patent's expiry[497].

Finally, there are demand-side policies directed at pharmacists. Every Member State has implemented controls for remuneration (especially through the regression of fixed fee margins) including via contractual arrangements. Moreover, governments encourage the dispensation of generic medicines over branded ones. The European Commission, in its final report on the pharmaceutical sector inquiry, concluded that countries that require pharmacists to dispense generics are more likely to have an earlier generic entry in the market and consequently achieve higher savings.

It is now necessary to talk about the greatest consequence that the various nationwide regulations on pharmaceuticals price cause at the European single market level: parallel trade, the main response to international price discrimination.

Parallel trade refers to the

> *(...) legal importation of a patented product from one country where it is legally marketed into a second country where the patent holder also markets that product but without authorisation of the patent holder*[498].

Parallel trade can regard all types of goods, but it is particularly the case with pharmaceuticals because of the highly regulated distribution of medicines. Indeed, as we have seen, the medicine prices sector can be

---

[496] The WHO defines OTC as "*a pharmaceutical product, drug, or medicinal specialty whose dispensing or administration does not require medical authorization, and it can be used by the consumers under its own initiative and responsibility to prevent, relieve or to treat symptoms or mild diseases and that its use, in the form, conditions and authorized dosages are safe for the consumer*".

[497] European Parliament, *Differences*, 48-49.

[498] Panos Kanavos and Joan Costa-Font, "Pharmaceutical Parallel Trade in Europe: Stakeholder and Competition Effects", *Economic Policy* 20, no. 44 (2005): 751-798, https://EconPapers.repec.org/RePEc:bla:ecpoli:v:20:y:2005:i:44:p:751-798.

easily manipulated by domestic politicians, but, at the same time, it is also influenced by the economic power of the pharmaceutical industry, especially because big companies are big taxpayers and providers of qualified workplaces. For these reasons, parallel trade is an important issue in the Union and constitutes a multibillion euro business[499].

This practice, which has the purpose of gaining profits from price discriminations across Member States, is illegal in most parts of the world, but not in the European Union, as part of the move to a single market of pharmaceuticals. Thus, over the years, medicinal products have been purchased in Member States at low prices and re-sold in higher-priced European countries through parallel trading activities.

An important part of the patchwork of the EU's medicines regulation is the jurisprudence of the Court of Justice of the European Union (CJEU). As we discussed in the legal analysis, the application and the defence of parallel trade practices has been mainly made through the decisions of the CJEU. During the last 35 years, the Court has applied the principle of the free movement of goods to fight against unjustified domestic restrictions to imports/exports which impede parallel trade and constitute barriers to the single market. Furthermore, the Court imposed the principle of Community exhaustion of Intellectual Property Rights (IPR) within the Union, implying that if IPR are exhausted by the first sale in one Member State, they must also be exhausted in all the other EU countries.

In response, research-based companies have resorted to dual-pricing strategies and supply quota systems in order to reduce or discourage parallel trade. However, both these strategies, under certain conditions, may contravene competition law.

Therefore, the combination of pharmaceuticals' price differences across Member States, competition policy that constrains how companies respond to parallel trade, the inability of the industry to use IPR to prevent the resale of its products, and the jurisprudence of the CJEU have fostered the parallel trade of medicines within the Union.

It has been stressed that the decisions of the CJEU, especially in relation to cases having IPR and market access as objects, have not so far been presented with detailed evidence about the economic and social effects of parallel trade as a whole[500].

---

499 Thomas N. Bart, "Parallel Trade of Pharmaceuticals: a Review of Legal, Economic, and Political Aspects", *Value in Health* 11, no. 5 (September – October 2008): 996-1005, https://doi.org/10.1111/j.1524-4733.2008.00339.x.

500 Dermot Glynn, "The effects of parallel trade on affordable access to medicines", *Eurohealth* 15, no. 2 (2009): 1-4.

Indeed, opinions on the impact of parallel trade are heterogeneous, with different researchers producing very different results and conclusions, often contradictory.

Economic studies have been advanced and conducted in relation to both sides of the debate. For example, there are studies affirming that patients can take advantage of this practice because the research-based industry is induced to lowering the prices of its products in order to keep its market share [501] (whereas other studies have concluded the exact opposite [502]). Proponents and policy makers in some Member States perceived parallel trade as a cost-containment mechanism, affirming that parallel trade offers savings to health insurers and consumers by increasing the affordability of high priced pharmaceuticals[503]. For these reasons, this practice has in some cases been encouraged[504].

By contrast, it is also thought that parallel trade is a key factor undermining the competitiveness of the sector in the Union by decreasing revenue flows, reducing innovation potential[505], and discouraging R&D, thus diminishing product quality and future research[506]. In this regard, some studies found a correlation between the rise of parallel imports and the collapse of the European pharmaceutical industry[507].

In addition, some studies pointed out that the subjects who benefit mostly from parallel trade are not patients, companies, health insurers or

---

[501] Mattias Ganslandt and Keith E. Maskus, "Parallel imports and pricing of pharmaceutical products: evidence from the European Union", *Journal of Health Economics* 23 (July 2004): 1035-1057, https://doi.org/10.1016/j.jhealeco.2004.03.005.

[502] Kanavos and Vandoros, "Competition".

[503] Reza Ahmadi and B. Rachel Yang, "Parallel Imports: Challenges for Unauthorized Distribution Channels", *Marketing Science* 19, no. 3 (August 2000): 279-294, https://doi.org/10.1287/mksc.19.3.279.11799.

[504] Peter West and James Mahon, *Benefits to Payers and Patients From Parallel Trade* (York: York Health Economics Consortium, 2003). See also, Panos Kanavos et al., *The Economic Impact of Pharmaceutical Parallel Trade in European Union Member States: A Stakeholder Analysis,* Special Research Paper (London: LSE Health and Social Care, January 2004), http://www.lse.ac.uk/LSEHealthAndSocialCare/pdf/Workingpapers/Paper.pdf.

[505] Stefan Szymanski, Tommaso Valletti and Gabrielle Demange, "Parallel Trade, Price Discrimination, Investment and Price Caps", *Economic Policy* 20, no. 44 (October 2005): 705-749, http://www.jstor.org/stable/3601057.

[506] See, for instance, Kanavos et al., *Economic Impact.*

[507] Jacob Arfwedson, *Re-importation (Parallel Trade) in Pharmaceuticals, Policy Report #182* (Lewisville: Institute for Policy Innovation, 2004), https://www.ipi.org/docLib/PR182-ParallelTrade.pdf-OpenElement.pdf.

third-party payers, but only parallel importers themselves[508]. Thus, parallel activities do not lead to significant savings for healthcare budgets, and this is true also because parallel traded products are usually priced quite closely to the corresponding nationally sourced ones[509].

Nevertheless, one of the other unintended consequences of parallel trade is that it can lead to shortages in exporting countries, due to medicines being exported to higher priced countries[510]. In order to avoid periodic shortages, the European legislator amended Article 81 of the Community Code Directive with the aim of facilitating the continuous supply of medicines within Member States. Nevertheless, other supply shortages, especially in markets with a great number of parallel traded drugs, were registered even after the implementation of the above-mentioned rule[511].

As already underlined, patients in lower income Member States have to wait for significant periods after new medicines are marketed elsewhere, reducing patient access to new drugs in the low-income countries[512].

For its part, the pharmaceutical industry, which has always fought against parallel trade, has repeatedly stated that the volatile activities of wholesalers result in an unpredictability of demand and complicated supply chain problems, undermining the effective allocation of resources and the consequent ability to ensure the appropriate level of stock necessary to meet patients' needs in each country[513].

The last undeniable problem that parallel trade involves is the increase in the risk of counterfeiting and the number of falsified medicines. Indeed, criminals have a greater opportunity to disguise counterfeit medicines,

---

[508] Kanavos et al., *Economic Impact.*

[509] Panos Kanavos and Stacey Kowal, "Does pharmaceutical parallel trade serve the objectives of cost control?", *Eurohealth* 14, no. 2 (2008): 22-26, http://www.lse.ac.uk/LSEHealthAndSocialCare/pdf/eurohealth/VOL14N2/Kanavos%20and%20Kowal.pdf.

[510] See, for example, Sally E. Gainsbury, "NHS drug shortage looms as pound falls", *Health Services Journal*, January 22, 2009.

[511] Glynn, "Effects", 2.

[512] Patricia M. Danzon, Y. Richard Wang, Liang Wang, "The impact of price regulation on the launch delay of new drugs – evidence from twenty-five major markets in the 1990s", *Health Economics* 14, no. 3 (September 2005): 269-292, https://doi.org/10.1002/hec.931.

[513] European Parliament, *Differences.*

given the practice of parallel traders to repackage pharmaceuticals in order to promote their sale in the destination countries[514].

It is quite obvious that the diversity of such visions and conclusions of the above-mentioned economic studies can be caused by the different interests, often conflicting, of the studies' sponsors. This means that further research is needed in order to investigate this field in the most objective manner possible, after evaluation methods have been standardised and the availability and quality of information have been increased[515].

Diversity can also be found in the proposals of the possible solutions that may be useful to correct the current panorama. Some propose a common European price scheme for new medicines in order to derive a single solution for many common challenges and consequently make European prices more transparent[516]. On the contrary, others affirm that a single EU price would reduce both the profits derived from the sale of branded medicines and their affordability, thereby limiting patient access[517].

Given all these conclusions, the CJEU, in some of its recent judgments[518], has also questioned some of the legal principles at the basis of the European pharmaceuticals' parallel trade. This latest fact could suggest the beginning of a policy change; however, this possibility and the ways in which this departure could take place remain partially unclear[519].

There are other problems related to price differences applied by the various regulations in force in the Member States. Among these we can mention the lack of transparency in the negotiations and in the decision-making processes undertaken by the domestic competent authorities. In particular, companies have repeatedly expressed concerns about the fact that some pricing and reimbursement decisions in Europe are extremely

---

514 J. Davies and D. Taylor, *Reducing the threat of medicines counterfeiting in the EU* (London: The School of Pharmacy, University of London, 2009).

515 Bart, "Parallel Trade".

516 Garattini, Curto and Freemantle, "Pharmaceutical".

517 Glynn, "Effects".

518 See, for example, Joined Cases C-2/01 P and C-3/01 P, Bundesverband der Arzneimittel-Importeure eV and Commission of the European Communities v. Bayer AG, 2004 E.C.R. I-00023, ECLI:EU:C:2004:2; Or Case C-53/03, Synetairismos Farmakopoion Aitolias & Akarnanias (Syfait) and Others v. GlaxoSmithKline plc and GlaxoSmithKline AEVE, 2005 E.C.R. I-04609, ECLI:EU:C:2005:333.

519 Claudia Desogus, "Competition and innovation in the EU regulation of pharmaceuticals, the case of parallel trade", *European Journal of Law and Economics* 34, no. 2 (October 2012): 423, https://doi.org/10.1007/s10657-012-9302-y.

opaque. Indeed, Member States use vague and ill-defined concepts without further specification or explanation, also contravening in this way the requirements of objectivity and verifiability imposed by the Transparency Directive. In this regard, enhancing cross-border collaboration between domestic regulators (e.g. with common data sets and common HTA methodologies), establishing joint evaluations on the impact of pricing and reimbursement practices and exchanging experiences between Member States are probably the best and most effective solutions to increase certainty. Some companies have suggested setting up early dialogues between decision-makers and companies to clarify the expected value of new medicines and the required proof needed to demonstrate it[520].

In conclusion, although the future is inherently uncertain, what is clear is that cost pressures on national healthcare budgets will increase due to the demographic evolution towards an older population, the rise in the incidence of certain diseases (such as cancer, dementia and diabetes) and the growing costs associated with the technological progress of innovative pharmaceuticals[521].

For these reasons, the most probable situation in the future will be the enhancement of collaborations on value for money regimes. This hypothesis is supported by the recent approval by the European Parliament of the Commission's proposal for a new Regulation on the HTA. Value-based pricing is a helpful means to make the use of the economic resources designated to finance healthcare more effective, keeping prices down and releasing funds that could be used to provide better patient access to medicinal products. Moreover, given that diversity of approach is a fact of life in Member States, it is unlikely that we will see any attempts to introduce Union-wide harmonising legislation on prices and reimbursements in the near future. Nevertheless, interest in voluntary cooperation is an increasingly shared feeling, and therefore it is probable that the principles resulting from such collaborations will be incorporated in guidelines and other soft-law instruments, which will offer more scope for flexibility and for balancing European and national interests[522].

---

520 European Commission, *Pharmaceutical Sector Inquiry,* 492-494.
521 Gregson et al., "Pricing Medicines".
522 Hancher, "EU Pharmaceuticals Market", 680-682.

CONCLUSIONS

In this long journey we have analysed the current system of pharmaceuticals regulation within the European Union. The entire panorama is characterised by two different levels of competences, often conflicting, which interact with each other: the responsibility of the Member States to organise their own healthcare systems, and the European Union's competence for the creation and development of the single market. Given that it is difficult to keep policy areas fully separated, European institutions have indirectly expanded their role over time despite their limited competence on healthcare issues. The result is a patchwork of rules and roles in which the main actors are the European legislator, with its hard-law, the CJEU, with its jurisprudence, and the instruments of new governance in the guise of networks and other forms of cooperation between Member States. Moreover, the European Parliament and the Council, after the entering into force of the Lisbon Treaty, gained the explicit competence to adopt measures setting high quality targets for medicinal products to help Member States to achieve common safety standards[523], especially where domestic standards would otherwise prevent a high level of human health protection from being achieved[524].

In this regard, first of all, we saw the regulatory developments and the resulting current measures introduced to harmonise certain aspects of the pharmaceuticals' lifecycles, from clinical trials to pharmacovigilance.

Subsequently, we discussed how the CJEU, through its judgments, set policy directions especially on the basis of atypical cases within the principles of the free movement of goods, competition law and, to some extent, fundamental rights. Finally, to complete the legal analysis, a quick look was given at the various soft law instruments that, through a prevalent voluntary adherence system, help Member States to coordinate their policies and practices in order to improve human healthcare.

We then discussed the economic and social consequences that the market fragmentation linked to disparities in national pricing and reimbursement schemes creates. Indeed, there are many domestic health

---

[523] TFEU, Article 168(4)(c).

[524] TFEU, Declaration on Article 168(4)(c) of the Treaty on the Functioning of the European Union.

schemes within each European country, and the pricing and reimbursement of pharmaceuticals are subject to very different rules across the Union. In particular, significant inequalities in patient access to medicines exist between EU citizens. We saw that the reasons for this problem can be of a double nature: the limited financial resources of middle-income Member States, which are unable to reimburse certain drugs; and the lack or inadequacy of the use of health technology assessments in order to decide which medicinal products, more or less cost-efficient, can efficiently be reimbursed or not.

Finally, the last topic examined concerned the different techniques used by the national regulators to establish the price of medicines, the mechanisms of cost containment applied to control public expenditure and the consequences of such price differentiations across the Union.

The different ways in which Member States organise their healthcare systems create a dilemma to achieve a single market of pharmaceuticals in the Union. Since the beginning of the first communitarian directives on medicinal products, the Commission has tried to create this single market in order to make European Union the pharmaceutical industry's natural home. It has been repeatedly argued[525] that this single market would enable the ultimate goal of making authorised medicines accessible to all patients in a fast, safe and sustainable manner. This achievement is made even more difficult because of the financial crisis, the rising costs of health technologies, an increasingly old population and the growth of some chronic diseases.

Given the whole situation, what will be the direction of travel in the future?

In this regard, three different scenarios for future developments can be presented.

First, it could be that the European institutions, in particular the Commission, start strong policies to overcome the diversity of national health systems through harmonising legislations in order to achieve, to the greatest extent possible, equal access to healthcare for all EU citizens. From a legal point of view, an amendment to the Treaties would probably be necessary for such a wide integration, given that the unanimity of the Council Members is required to issue decisions concerning the harmonisation of national legislations in the field of social security (including healthcare). Obviously, unanimity is very hard to obtain in an

---

[525] See, for example, European Commission, *Communication.*

EU composed of 28 (27 after Brexit) Member States. Still, even if such an amendment occurs, a purely regulatory role is simply not enough in a Union in which Member States have different per capita spending on healthcare and different measures to control the rising costs of health. This means that, before regulatory harmonisation, there is a need to harmonise Member States' financial capabilities.

Therefore, this scenario is extremely unlikely because there are no signs of such intentions, and there would be a need for important redistributive actions at EU-level and strong financial input from the Union (which is not realistic, also given that the Health Programme for 2014–2020 only has a fund of around 450 million euros[526])[527].

The second scenario provides for the maintenance of the status quo. In practice, the current panorama would remain unchanged, with concrete EU action mainly directed to assisting the progress of fiscal consolidation, ensuring free movement and fostering soft law mechanisms for the promotion of Member States' cooperation in the healthcare sector. We should remember, for example, the Commission's continuous support and push for cooperation and an exchange of information between national competent bodies, third-party payers and the pharmaceutical industry in HTA. Indeed, it is felt to be necessary to develop broadly acceptable HTA mechanisms, and a more consistent and sustainable HTA approach within the Union in order to define, *inter alia*, the depth of coverage of different Member States. Such a meeting of information and best practices could help Member States to compare other countries' levels of health coverage with their own and thus assist them in planning their own costs accordingly[528].

Given the current situation and the recent approval by the European Parliament of the Commission's proposal on a new Regulation on the HTA, this second scenario seems quite probable.

Finally, the last imaginable scenario could be the push towards disintegration. In this case, the European redistributive mechanisms will weaken further, thus making the Union simply a free trade zone with an

---

526 See "EU Health Programme", European Commission, accessed November 28, 2018, https://ec.europa.eu/health/funding/programme_en.

527 Tomislav Sokol and Nikola Mijatović, "EU Health Law and Policy and the Eurozone crisis", in *Research Handbook on EU Health Law and Policy,* eds. Tamara K. Hervey, Calum Alasdair Young and Louise E. Bishop (Cheltenham: Edward Elgar Publishing, 2017), 311-314.

528 Ibid.

insignificant role in other areas of human activity. In this situation, common policy may only be maintained through intergovernmental voluntary cooperation. However, the overall political climate in a (partly) disintegrating EU could be an obstacle to strong cooperation between domestic healthcare systems. Therefore, it would be hard to speak of a real EU health law and policy[529].

Moreover, some anti-European political exponents have already advocated this possible future situation; some of them are also gaining an ever more popular consensus.

Therefore, in conclusion, it is difficult to establish with certainty which of the last two scenarios will prevail, meaning that the future remains uncertain.

---

[529] Ibid.

LIST OF ABBREVIATIONS

ADRs	Adverse Drug Reactions
ATMPs	Advanced Therapy Medicinal Products
BSE	Bovine Spongiform Encephalopathy
BWP	Biologics Working Party
CAPs	Centrally Authorised Products
CAT	Committee for Advanced Therapies
CbP	Cost-based Pricing
CFREU	Charter of Fundamental Rights of the European Union
CHMP	Committee for Medicinal Products for Human Use
CJEU	Court of Justice of the European Union
CMDh	Coordination Group for Mutual Recognition and Decentralised Procedures – Human
COMP	Committee for Orphan Medicinal Products
CPMP	Committee for Proprietary Medicinal Products
CSRs	Country-Specific Recommendations
DoH	Declaration of Helsinki
DPV	*Deutsche Parkinson Vereinigung* eV
EC	European Community
ECHR	European Convention on Human Rights and Fundamental Freedoms
EDQM	European Directorate for the Quality of Medicines
EEA	European Economic Area
EEC	European Economic Community
EGE	European Group on Ethics in Science and New Technologies
EMA	European Medicines Agency
EMEA	European Agency for the Evaluation of Medicinal Products
ERP	External Reference Pricing
ERNs	European Reference Networks
EU	European Union
EUnetHTA	European Network for Health Technology Assessment
FRA	Fundamental Rights Agency

GCP	Good Clinical Practice
GDP	Good Distribution Practice
GMP	Good Manufacturing Practices
GSK	GlaxoSmithKline
GVP	Good Pharmacovigilance Practices
GxP	Generic Good Practice
HMPC	Committee for Herbal Medicinal Products
HTA	Health Technology Assessment
HTAi	Health Technology Assessment international
ICH	International Conference on Harmonisation of Technical Requirements for Registration of Pharmaceuticals for Human Use
INHTA	International Network of Agencies of Health Technology Assessment
IPR	Intellectual Property Rights
IT	Information Technology
MEP	Member of the European Parliament
MRP	Mutual Recognition Procedure
MS	Member State
NAPs	Nationally Authorised Products
NGO	Non-governmental Organisation
NHS	National Health Service
OMC	Open Method of Coordination
OMCLs	Official Medicines Control Laboratories
OOP	Out-of-pocket
OTC	Over-the-counter
PDCO	Paediatric Committee
PIPs	Paediatric Investigation Plans
PLD	Product Liability Directive
PPRS	Pharmaceutical Price Regulation Scheme
PRAC	Pharmacovigilance Risk Assessment Committee
PSURs	Periodic Safety Update Reports
R&D	Research and Development
RbP	Reference-based Price
RMP	Risk Management Plan
RMS	Reference Member State
SPC	Summary of Product Characteristics
STAMP	Safe and Timely Access to Medicines for Patients
SUSARs	Suspected Unexpected Serious Adverse Reactions
TEU	Treaty on European Union
TFEU	Treaty on the Functioning of the European Union

VbP	Value-based Price
WHO	World Health Organisation

Figure 1-1 The EU-wide common logo for identifying legal online pharmacies

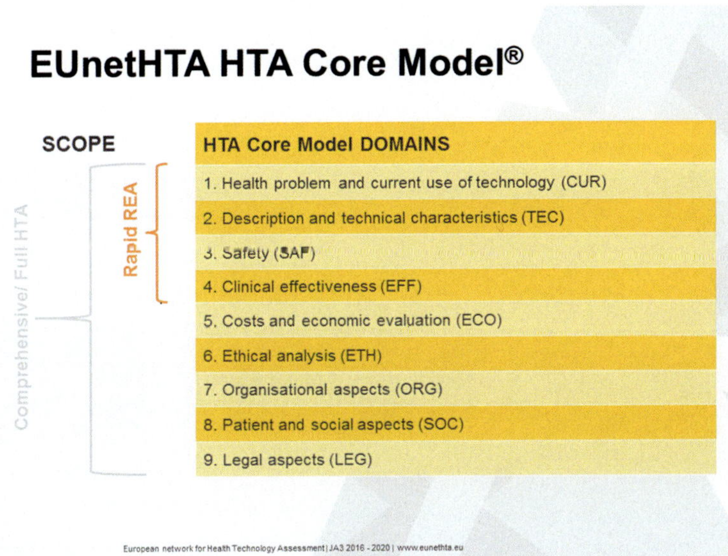

Figure 4-1 EUnetHTA HTA Core model® Domains

The Mentioned EU Directives, Regulations and Treaties

EU Charters

Charter of Fundamental Rights of the European Union, 2012 O.J. (C 326) 392, https://eur-lex.europa.eu/legal-content/EN/TXT/?uri=celex:12012P/TXT.

EU Directives

Council Directive 65/65/EEC of 26 January 1965 on the approximation of provisions laid down by Law, Regulation or Administrative Action relating to proprietary medicinal products, 1965 O.J. 22 369, https://eur-lex.europa.eu/eli/dir/1965/65/oj.

Council Directive 75/318/EEC of 20 May 1975 on the approximation of the laws of Member States relating to analytical, pharmaco-toxicological and clinical standards and protocols in respect of the testing of proprietary medicinal products, 1975 O.J. (L 147) 1, http://data.europa.eu/eli/dir/1975/318/oj.

Second Council Directive 75/319/EEC of 20 May 1975 on the approximation of provisions laid down by law, regulation or administrative action relating to proprietary medicinal products, 1975 O.J. (L 147) 13, http://data.europa.eu/eli/dir/1975/319/oj.

Council Directive 83/570/EEC of 26 October 1983 amending Directives 65/65/EEC, 75/318/EEC and 75/319/EEC on the approximation of provisions laid down by law, regulation or administrative action relating to proprietary medicinal products, 1983 O.J. (L 332) 1, http://data.europa.eu/eli/dir/1983/570/oj.

Council Directive 85/374/EEC of 25 July 1985 on the approximation of the laws, regulations and administrative provisions of the Member States concerning liability for defective products, 1985 O.J. (L 210) 29, http://data.europa.eu/eli/dir/1985/374/oj.

Council Directive 87/21/EEC of 22 December 1986 amending Directive 65/65/EEC on the approximation of provisions laid down by law, regulation or administrative action relating to proprietary medicinal products; 1987 O.J. (L 15) 36, http://data.europa.eu/eli/dir/1987/21/oj.

Council Directive 87/22/EEC of 22 December 1986 on the approximation of national measures relating to the placing on the market of high-technology medicinal products, particularly those derived from biotechnology; 1987 O.J. (L 15) 38, http://data.europa.eu/eli/dir/1987/22/oj.

Council Directive 89/105/EEC of 21 December 1988 relating to the transparency of measures regulating the prices of medicinal products for human use and their inclusion in the scope of national health insurance systems; 1989 O.J. (L 40) 8, http://data.europa.eu/eli/dir/1989/105/oj.

Council Directive 89/342/EEC of 3 May 1989 extending the scope of Directives 65/65/EEC and 75/319/EEC and laying down additional provisions for immunological medicinal products consisting of vaccines, toxins or serums and allergens; 1989 O.J. (L 142) 14, http://data.europa.eu/eli/dir/1989/342/oj.

Council Directive 89/381/EEC of 14 June 1989 extending the scope of Directives 65/65/EEC and 75/319/EEC on the approximation of provisions laid down by Law, Regulation or Administrative Action relating to proprietary medicinal products and laying down special provisions for medicinal products derived from human blood or human plasma; 1989 O.J. (L 181) 44, http://data.europa.eu/eli/dir/1989/381/oj.

Commission Directive 91/356/EEC of 13 June 1991 laying down the principles and guidelines of good manufacturing practice for medicinal products for human use; 1991 O.J. (L 193) 30, http://data.europa.eu/eli/dir/1991/356/oj.

Commission Directive 91/412/EEC of 23 July 1991 laying down the principles and guidelines of good manufacturing practice for veterinary medicinal products; 1991 O.J. (L 228) 70, http://data.europa.eu/eli/dir/1991/412/oj.

Council Directive 92/25/EEC of 31 March 1992 on the wholesale distribution of medicinal products for human use; 1992 O.J. (L 113) 1, http://data.europa.eu/eli/dir/1992/25/oj.

Council Directive 92/26/EEC of 31 March 1992 concerning the classification for the supply of medicinal products for human use; 1992 O.J. (L 113) 5, http://data.europa.eu/eli/dir/1992/26/oj.

Council Directive 92/27/EEC of 31 March 1992 on the labelling of medicinal products for human use and on package leaflets; 1992 O.J. (L 113) 8, http://data.europa.eu/eli/dir/1992/27/oj.

Council Directive 92/28/EEC of 31 March 1992 on the advertising of medicinal products for human use; 1992 O.J. (L 113) 13, http://data.europa.eu/eli/dir/1992/28/oj.

Council Directive 92/73/EEC of 22 September 1992 widening the scope of Directives 65/65/EEC and 75/319/EEC on the approximation of provisions laid down by Law, Regulation or Administrative Action relating to medicinal products and laying down additional provisions on homeopathic medicinal products; 1992 O.J. (L 297) 8, http://data.europa.eu/eli/dir/1992/73/oj.

Council Directive 93/39/EEC of 14 June 1993 amending Directives 65/65/EEC, 75/318/EEC and 75/319/EEC in respect of medicinal products; 1993 O.J. (L 214) 22, http://data.europa.eu/eli/dir/1993/39/oj.

Directive 2001/20/EC of the European Parliament and of the Council of 4 April 2001 on the approximation of the laws, regulations and administrative provisions of the member states relating to the implementation of good clinical practice in the conduct of clinical trials on medicinal products for human use; 2001 O.J. (L 121) 34, http://data.europa.eu/eli/dir/2001/20/oj.

Directive 2001/83/EC of the European Parliament and of the Council of 6 November 2001 on the community code relating to medicinal products for human use; 2001 O.J. (L 311) 67, http://data.europa.eu/eli/dir/2001/83/oj.

Commission Directive 2003/94/EC of 8 October 2003 laying down the principles and guidelines of good manufacturing practice in respect of medicinal products for human use and investigational medicinal products for human use; 2003 O.J. (L 262) 22, http://data.europa.eu/eli/dir/2003/94/oj.

Directive 2004/24/EC of the European Parliament and of the Council of 31 March 2004 amending, as regards traditional herbal medicinal products, Directive 2001/83/EC on the Community code relating to medicinal products for human use; 2004 O.J. (L 136) 85, http://data.europa.eu/eli/dir/2004/24/oj.

Directive 2004/27/EC of the European Parliament and of the Council of 31 March 2004 amending Directive 2001/83/EC on the Community code relating to medicinal products for human use; 2004 O.J. (L 136) 34, http://data.europa.eu/eli/dir/2004/27/oj.

Directive 2010/63/EU of the European Parliament and of the Council of 22 September 2010 on the protection of animals used for scientific purposes; 2010 O.J. (L 276) 33, http://data.europa.eu/eli/dir/2010/63/oj.

Directive 2010/84/EU of the European Parliament and of the Council of 15 December 2010 amending, as regards pharmacovigilance, Directive 2001/83/EC on the Community code relating to medicinal products for human use; 2010 O.J. (L 348) 74, http://data.europa.eu/eli/dir/2010/84/oj.

Directive 2011/24/EU of the European Parliament and of the Council of 9 March 2011 on the application of patients' rights in cross-border healthcare; 2011 O.J. (L 88) 45, http://data.europa.eu/eli/dir/2011/24/oj.

Directive 2011/62/EU of the European Parliament and of the Council of 8 June 2011 amending Directive 2001/83/EC on the Community code relating to medicinal products for human use, as regards the prevention of the entry into the legal supply chain of falsified medicinal products; 2011 O.J. L (174) 74, http://data.europa.eu/eli/dir/2011/62/oj.

Directive 2012/26/EU of the European Parliament and of the Council of 25 October 2012 amending Directive 2001/83/EC as regards pharmacovigilance; 2012 O.J. (L 299) 1, http://data.europa.eu/eli/dir/2012/26/oj.

EU Regulations

Council Regulation (EEC) No. 2309/93 of 22 July 1993 laying down Community procedures for the authorisation and supervision of medicinal products for human and veterinary use and establishing a European Agency for the Evaluation of Medicinal Products; 1993 O.J. (L 214) 1, https://ec.europa.eu/health/sites/health/files/files/eudralex/vol-1/reg_1993_2309/reg_1993_2309_en.pdf.

Council Regulation (EC) No. 297/95 of 10 February 1995 on fees payable to the European Agency for the Evaluation of Medicinal Products; 1995 O.J. (L 35) 1, http://data.europa.eu/eli/reg/1995/297/2018-04-01.

Regulation (EC) No. 141/2000 of the European Parliament and of the Council of 16 December 1999 on orphan medicinal products; 2000 O.J. (L 18) 1, http://data.europa.eu/eli/reg/2000/141/oj.

Regulation (EC) No. 726/2004 of the European Parliament and of the Council of 31 March 2004 laying down Community procedures for the authorisation and supervision of medicinal products for human and veterinary use and establishing a European Medicines Agency; 2004 O.J. (L 136) 1, http://data.europa.eu/eli/reg/2004/726/oj.

Regulation (EC) No. 1901/2006 of the European Parliament and of the Council of 12 December 2006 on medicinal products for paediatric use and amending Regulation (EEC) No. 1768/92, Directive 2001/20/EC, Directive 2001/83/EC and Regulation (EC) No. 726/2004; 2006 O.J. (L 378) 1, http://data.europa.eu/eli/reg/2006/1901/oj.

Regulation (EC) No. 1394/2007 of the European Parliament and of the Council of 13 November 2007 on advanced therapy medicinal products and amending Directive 2001/83/EC and Regulation (EC) No. 726/2004; 2007 O.J. (L 324) 121, http://data.europa.eu/eli/reg/2007/1394/oj.

Regulation (EU) No. 1235/2010 of the European Parliament and of the Council of 15 December 2010 amending, as regards pharmacovigilance of medicinal products for human use, Regulation (EC) No. 726/2004 laying down Community procedures for the authorisation and supervision of medicinal products for human and veterinary use and establishing a European Medicines Agency, and Regulation (EC) No. 1394/2007 on advanced therapy medicinal products; 2010 O.J. (L 348) 1, http://data.europa.eu/eli/reg/2010/1235/oj.

Regulation (EU) No. 1027/2012 of the European Parliament and of the Council of 25 October 2012 amending Regulation (EC) No. 726/2004 as regards pharmacovigilance; 2012 O.J. (L 316) 38, http://data.europa.eu/eli/reg/2012/1027/oj.

Regulation (EU) No. 282/2014 of the European Parliament and of the Council of 11 March 2014 on the establishment of a third Programme for the Union's action in the field of health (2014-2020) and repealing Decision No.1350/2007/EC, 2014 O.J. (L 86) 1, http://data.europa.eu/eli/reg/2014/282/oj.

Regulation (EU) No. 536/2014 of the European Parliament and of the Council of 16 April 2014 on clinical trials on medicinal products for human use, and repealing Directive 2001/20/EC; 2014 O.J. (L 158) 1, http://data.europa.eu/eli/reg/2014/536/oj.

Regulation (EU) No. 658/2014 of the European Parliament and of the Council of 15 May 2014 on fees payable to the European Medicines Agency for the conduct of pharmacovigilance activities in respect of medicinal products for human use; 2014 O.J. (L 189) 112, http://data.europa.eu/eli/reg/2014/658/2018-02-12.

Regulation (EU) 2017/745 of the European Parliament and of the Council of 5 April 2017 on medical devices, amending Directive 2001/83/EC, Regulation (EC) No. 178/2002 and Regulation (EC) No. 1223/2009 and repealing Council Directives 90/385/EEC and 93/42/EEC; 2017 O.J. (L 117) 1, http://data.europa.eu/eli/reg/2017/745/oj.

EU Treaties

Treaty on European Union, 1992 O.J. (C 191) 1.

Treaty of Amsterdam amending the Treaty on European Union, the Treaties establishing the European Communities and certain related acts-Final Act, 1997 O.J. (C 340) 115, https://eur-lex.europa.eu/legal-content/EN/TXT/?uri=CELEX%3A11997D%2FAFI.

Treaty of Lisbon amending the Treaty on European Union and the Treaty establishing the European Community, 2007 O.J. (C 306) 1, https://eur-lex.europa.eu/legal-content/en/TXT/?uri=CELEX%3A12007L%2FTXT.

Consolidated version of the Treaty on European Union, 2012 O.J. (C 326) 13, https://eur-lex.europa.eu/legal-content/en/TXT/?uri=CELEX%3A12012M%2FTXT.

Consolidated version of the Treaty on the Functioning of the European Union, 2012 O.J. (C 326) 47, https://eur-lex.europa.eu/legal-content/EN/TXT/?uri=celex%3A12012E%2FTXT.

BIBLIOGRAPHY

Abelson, Julia, Mita Giacomini, Pascale Lehoux, and Francois-Pierre Gauvin. "Bringing 'the public' into health technology assessment and coverage public decisions: From principles to practice". *Health Policy* 82, no. 1 (June 2007): 37-50. https://doi.org/10.1016/j.healthpol.2006.07.009.

Ahmadi, Reza and B. Rachel Yang. "Parallel Imports: Challenges for Unauthorized Distribution Channels". *Marketing Science* 19, no. 3 (August 2000): 279-294. https://doi.org/10.1287/mksc.19.3.279.11799.

Alasdair Young, Calum. "Fundamental rights and EU health law and policy". In *Research Handbook on EU Health Law and Policy,* edited by Tamara K. Hervey, Calum Alasdair Young and Louise E. Bishop, 82-110. Cheltenham: Edward Elgar Publishing, 2017.

Allen, Nicola, Lawrence Liberti, Stuart R. Walker, and Sam Salek. "A Comparison of Reimbursement Recommendations by European HTA Agencies: Is There Opportunity for Further Alignment?". *Frontiers in Pharmacology* 8, (June 2017): 384. https://doi.org/10.3389/fphar.2017.00384.

Almunia, Joaquin. "Commission fines Lundbeck and other pharma companies for delaying market entry of generic medicines: statement by Vice-President Almunia". European Commission, last update February 19, 2018. http://europa.eu/rapid/press-release_SPEECH-13-553_en.htm.

Altenstetter, Christa. *Medical devices: European Union policymaking and the implementation of health and patient safety in France.* New Brunswick, N.J.: Transaction Publishers, 2008.

Alter, Karen. *The European Court's Political Power: Selected Essays.* Oxford: Oxford University Press, 2009.

Arfwedson, Jacob. *Re-importation (Parallel Trade) in Pharmaceuticals, Policy Report #182.* Lewisville: Institute for Policy Innovation, 2004. https://www.ipi.org/docLib/PR182-ParallelTrade.pdf-OpenElement.pdf.

Barnard, Catherine and Steve Peers. *European Union Law*. Oxford: Oxford University Press, 2017.

Bart, Thomas N. "Parallel Trade of Pharmaceuticals: a Review of Legal, Economic, and Political Aspects". *Value in Health* 11, no. 5

(September – October 2008): 996-1005. https://doi.org/10.1111/j.1524-4733.2008.00339.x.

Battista, Renaldo N. "Towards a paradigm for technology assessment". In *The scientific basis of health services,* edited by Michael Peckham and Richard Smith, 11-18. London: BMJ Publishing Group, 1996.

Brekke, Kurt R., Ingrid Koenigbauer, and Odd Rune Straume. "Reference pricing of pharmaceuticals". *Journal of Health Economics* 26, no. 3 (2007): 613-642.

Busse, Reinhard, Jacques Orvain, Marcial Velasco, Matthias Perleth, Michael Drummond, Felix Gürtner, Torben Jørgensen et al. "Best Practice in undertaking and reporting health technology assessments: Working Group 4 Report". *International Journal of Technology Assessment in Health Care* 18, no. 2 (April 2002): 361-422.

Cavazza, Marianna and Claudio Jommi. "Stakeholders involvement by HTA Organisations: Why is so different?". *Health Policy* 105, no. 2-3 (May 2012): 236-245. https://doi.org/10.1016/j.healthpol.2012.01.012.

Ciani, Oriana, Rosanna Tarricone, and Aleksandra Torbica. "Diffusion and use of health technology assessment in policy making: What lessons for decentralised healthcare systems?". *Health Policy* 108, no. 2-3 (December 2012): 194-202.
https://doi.org/10.1016/j.healthpol.2012.09.017.

Council of the European Union. *Council conclusions on strengthening the balance in the pharmaceutical systems in the European Union and its Member States*. 2016 O.J. (C 296) 31.
https://publications.europa.eu/en/publication-detail/-/publication/b49097b2-5096-11e6-89bd-01aa75ed71a1/language-en.

Danzon, Patricia M., Y. Richard Wang, and Liang Wang. "The impact of price regulation on the launch delay of new drugs – evidence from twenty-five major markets in the 1990s". *Health Economics* 14, no. 3 (September 2005): 269-292. https://doi.org/10.1002/hec.931.

Davies J. and D. Taylor. *Reducing the threat of medicines counterfeiting in the EU*. London: The School of Pharmacy, University of London, 2009.

De Ruijter, Anniek. "*The Impediment of Health Laws. Values in the Constitutional Setting of the EU*". In *Research Handbook on EU Health Law and Policy,* edited by Tamara K. Hervey, Calum Alasdair Young and Louise E. Bishop, 479-495. Cheltenham: Edward Elgar Publishing, 2017.

De Ruijter, Anniek. "A silent revolution: the expansion of EU power in the field of human health. A rights-based analysis of EU health law and policy". PhD Thesis, University of Amsterdam, 2015.

Dehousse, Renaud. "Integration through law revisited: some thoughts on the juridification of the European political process". In *The Europeanisation of Law: The Legal Effects of European Integration,* edited by Francis Snyder, 15-30. Oxford: Hart Publishing, 2000.

Desogus, Claudia. "Competition and innovation in the EU regulation of pharmaceuticals, the case of parallel trade". *European Journal of Law and Economics* 34, no. 2 (October 2012): 423. https://doi.org/10.1007/s10657-012-9302-y.

Dylst, Pieter, Arnold G. Vulto, and Steven Simoens. "Reference pricing systems in Europe: characteristics and consequences". *Generics and Biosimilars Initiative Journal* 1, no. 3-4 (2012): 127-131. https://doi.org/10.5639/gabij.2012.0103-4.028.

Espín, Jaime and Joan Rovina. *Analysis of differences and commonalities in pricing and reimbursement systems in Europe, Final Report.* Brussels: European Commission, June 2007. https://ec.europa.eu/docsroom/documents/7605?locale=en.

EUnetHTA. *An analysis of HTA and reimbursement procedures in EUnetHTA partner countries: final report.* EUnetHTA WP7 research and analysis activity 1, 2017.

European Commission. *Communication from the Commission to the European Parliament, the Council, the European Economic and Social Committee and the Committee of the Regions: Safe, Innovative and Accessible Medicines: A Renewed Vision for the Pharmaceutical Sector*. COM (2008) 666 final. http://eurlex.europa.eu/LexUriServ/LexUriServ.do?uri=COM:2008:0666:FIN:en:PDF.

European Commission. *Pharmaceutical Sector Inquiry.* Final Report, European Commission, 2009. http://ec.europa.eu/competition/sectors/pharmaceuticals/inquiry/staff_working_paper_part1.pdf.

European Commission. *Pharmacovigilance related activities of Member States and the European Medicines Agency concerning medicinal products for human use (2012-2014).* Report from the Commission, COM (2016) 498 final, 2016. https://ec.europa.eu/health/sites/health/files/files/pharmacovigilance/pharmacovigilance-report-2012-2014_en.pdf.

European Commission. *Strengthening of the EU cooperation on Health Technology Assessment (HTA).* 2016. http://ec.europa.eu/smart-regulation/roadmaps/docs/2016_sante_144_health_technology_assessments_en.pdf.

European Medicines Agency. *The European regulatory system for medicines: A consistent approach to medicines regulation across the European Union*. EMA/716925/2016. https://www.ema.europa.eu/documents/leaflet/european-regulatory-system-medicines-european-medicines-agency-consistent-approach-medicines_en.pdf.

European Medicines Agency, and European Commission. "*Biosimilars in the EU. Information guide for healthcare professionals*". Last updated on April 27, 2017. http://www.ema.europa.eu/docs/en_GB/document_library/Leaflet/2017/05/WC500226648.pdf.

European Parliament, Directorate-General for Internal Policies. *Differences in Cost of and Access to pharmaceutical products in the EU*. Brussels, March 2011, 16. http://www.europarl.europa.eu/RegData/etudes/etudes/join/2011/451481/IPOL-ENVI_ET(2011)451481_EN.pdf.

European Parliament, Directorate General For Internal Policies. *EU Options for Improving Access to Medicines*. Workshop, Brussels, July 14, 2016. http://www.europarl.europa.eu/RegData/etudes/STUD/2016/587304/IPOL_STU(2016)587304_EN.pdf.

Fierlbeck, Katherine. "The changing contours of experimental governance in European health care". *Social Science & Medicine* 108, (May 2014): 90. https://doi.org/10.1016/j.socscimed.2014.02.040.

Fintel, Bara, Athena T. Samaras, and Edson Carias. "The Thalidomide Tragedy: Lessons for Drugs Safety and Regulation". *Helix Magazine*, Jun 28, 2009. https://helix.northwestern.edu/article/thalidomide-tragedy-lessons-drug-safety-and-regulation.

Freedman, Sandra. "Transformation or dilution: fundamental rights in the EU social space". *European Law Journal* 12, no. 1 (January 2006): 41. https://doi.org/10.1111/j.1468-0386.2006.00306.x.

Gainsbury, Sally E. "NHS drug shortage looms as pound falls". *Health Services Journal*, January 22, 2009.

Ganslandt, Mattias and Keith E. Maskus. "Parallel imports and pricing of pharmaceutical products: evidence from the European Union". *Journal of Health Economics* 23, (July 2004): 1035-1057. https://doi.org/10.1016/j.jhealeco.2004.03.005.

Ganslandt, Mattias and Keith Maskus. "Parallel Imports of Pharmaceutical Products in the European Union". Policy Research Working Paper Series, No. 2630, The World Bank, 2011. https://EconPapers.repec.org/RePEc:wbk:wbrwps:2630.

Garattini, Livio, Alessandro Curto, and Nick Freemantle. "Pharmaceutical Price Schemes in Europe: Time for a 'Continental' One?". *PharmacoEconomics* 34, no. 5 (May 2016): 423-426. https://doi.org/10.1007/s40273-015-0377-5.

Glynn, Dermot. "The effects of parallel trade on affordable access to medicines". *Eurohealth* 15, no. 2 (2009): 1-4.

Greer, Scott L. "Choosing Paths in European Union Health Policy: A Political Analysis of a Critical Juncture". *Journal of European Social Policy* 18, no. 3 (August 2008): 219-231.

Gregson, Nigel, Keiron Sparrowhawk, Josephine Mauskopf, and John Paul. "Pricing Medicines: Theory and Practice, Challenges and Opportunities". *Nature Review Drug Discovery* 4, no. 2 (February 2005): 121-130. https://doi.org/10.1038/nrd1633.

Grigoriadis, Lazaros Grigorios. "The Application of EU Competition Law in the Pharmaceutical Sector: The Case of Parallel Trade". *European Business Law Review* 25, no. 1 (2014): 141-201. https://ssrn.com/abstract=2206244.

Gurgula, Olga. "Restrictive Practices in Pharmaceutical Industry: Reverse Payment Agreements. Seeking for a Balance between Intellectual Property and Competition Law". *ICC Global Antitrust Review*, no. 5 (2012): 58-104. https://ssrn.com/abstract=2841884 or http://dx.doi.org/10.2139/ssrn.2841884.

Guy, Mary, and Wolf Sauter. "The History and Scope of EU Health Law and Policy". CCP Working Paper 16-2. Norwich: Centre for Competition Policy, University of East Anglia, 2016. http://competitionpolicy.ac.uk/documents/8158338/11320618/CCP+WP+16-2+complete.pdf.

Guy, Mary, and Wolf Sauter. "The History and Scope of EU Health Law and Policy". In *Research Handbook on EU Health Law and Policy,* edited by Tamara K. Hervey, Calum Alasdair Young and Louise E. Bishop, 17-35. Cheltenham: Edward Elgar Publishing, 2017.

Hancher, Leigh. "The EU Pharmaceuticals Market: Parameters and Pathways". In *Health Systems Governance in Europe: The Role of European Union Law and Policy*, edited by Elias Mossialos, Govin Permanand, Rita Baeten, and Tamara K. Hervey, 635-682. New York: Cambridge University Press, 2010.

Hancher, Leigh. "The European Community dimension: coordinating divergence". In *Regulating pharmaceuticals in Europe: striving for efficiency, equity and quality,* edited by Elias Mossialos, Monique Mrazek and Tom Walley, 55-79. Maidenhead: Open University Press, 2004.

Hancher, Leigh and Wolf Sauter. "A dose of competition: EU antitrust law in the pharmaceuticals sector". *Journal of Antitrust Enforcement* 4, no. 2 (October 2016): 381-410. https://doi.org/10.1093/jaenfo/jnw001.

Henshall, Chris, Logan Mardhani-Bayne, Katrine B. Frønsdal, and Marianne Klemp. "Interactions between health technology assessment, coverage, and regulatory processes: Emerging issues, goals, and opportunities". *International Journal of Technology Assessment in Health care* 27, no. 3 (July 2011): 253-260. https://doi.org/10.1017/S0266462311000262.

Hervey, Tamara K. "EU Health Law". In *European Union Law,* edited by Catherine Barnard and Steve Peers, 621-650. Oxford: Oxford University Press, 2014.

Hervey, Tamara K. and Jean V. McHale. *European Union Health Law: Themes and Implications.* Cambridge: Cambridge University Press, 2015.

Hervey, Tamara K. and Jean V. McHale. *Health law and the European Union.* Cambridge: Cambridge University Press, 2004.

Hervey, Tamara K. and Bart Vanhercke. "Health care and the EU: the law and policy patchwork". In *Health systems Governance in Europe: The Role of European Union Law and Policy,* edited by Elias Mossialos, Govin Permanand, Rita Baeten, and Tamara K. Hervey, 84-133. New York: Cambridge University Press, 2010.

Inglese, Marco. "*Unione Europea e sanità*". PhD diss., Università di Bologna, 2014.

Ioannides-Demos, Lisa L., Joseph E. Ibrahim, and John J. McNeil. "Reference-Based Pricing Schemes: Effect on Pharmaceutical Expenditure, Resource Utilisation and Health Outcomes". *Pharmacoeconomics* 20, no. 9 (August 2002): 577-591. https://doi.org/10.2165/00019053-200220090-00002.

Jackson, Emily. *Law and Regulation of Medicines.* Oxford: Hart Publishing, 2012.

Kanavos, Panos and Joan Costa-Font. "Pharmaceutical Parallel Trade in Europe: Stakeholder and Competition Effects". *Economic Policy* 20, no. 44 (2005): 751-798. https://EconPapers.repec.org/RePEc:bla:ecpoli:v:20:y:2005:i:44:p:751-798.

Kanavos, Panos, Joan Costa-i-Font, Sherry Merkur, and Marin Gemmill. *The Economic Impact of Pharmaceutical Parallel Trade in European Union Member States: A Stakeholder Analysis.* Special Research Paper. London: LSE Health and Social Care, January 2004.

.ra. *Five Years Down the Road: an Evaluation of the ing of the OMC in Social Policy Fields.* OSE, Briefing paper ember 2011.

'olfram. "European Union Health Care Policy". In *European ublic Health Policy – Regional and Global Trends*, edited by . Greer and Paulette Kurzer, 19-35. New York: Routledge,

Pierre-Louis. *International Cooperation, Convergence and onization of Pharmaceutical Regulations: A Global Perspective.* .emic Press, 2013.

, Jean. "Fundamental rights and health care". In *Health systems ›ernance in Europe: The Role of European Union Law and Policy,* .ted by Elias Mossialos, Govin Permanand, Rita Baeten, and Tamara . Hervey, 282-314. New York: Cambridge University Press, 2010.

.ee, Martin, Tamara K. Hervey, and Anna Gilmore. "Public Health ʾolicies". In *Health Systems Governance in Europe: The Role of European Union Law and Policy*, edited by Elias Mossialos, Govin Permanand, Rita Baeten, and Tamara K. Hervey, 231-281. New York: Cambridge University Press, 2010.

IcKee, Martin, and Elias Mossialos. "Health policy and European law: closing the gaps". *Public Health* 120, no. S1, (October 2006): 16-22. https://doi.org/10.1016/j.puhe.2006.07.008.

McKee, Martin, Elias Mossialos, and Paul Belcher. "The Influence of European Law on National Health Policy". *Journal of European Social Policy* 6, no. 4 (November 1996): 263.

Mossialos, Elias, Monique Mrazek, and Tom Walley. *Regulating pharmaceuticals in Europe: striving for efficiency, equity and quality.* Maidenhead: Open University Press, 2004.

Mossialos, Elias, Govin Permanand, Rita Baeten, and Tamara K. Hervey. *Health Systems Governance in Europe: The Role of European Union Law and Policy.* New York: Cambridge University Press, 2010.

Nielsen, Camilla Palmhøj, Sarah Wadmann Lauritsen, Finn Børlum Kristensen, Marie Louise Bistrup, Americo Cecchetti, and Eva Turk. "Involving stakeholders and developing a policy for stakeholder involvement in the European network for health technology assessment, EUnetHTA". *International Journal of Technology Assessment in Health Care* 25, no. S2 (December 2009): 84-91. https://doi.org/10.1017/S0266462309990729.

OECD Health Policy Studies. *Pharmaceutical Pricing Policies in a Global Market*. Paris: OECD Publishing, 2008.

http://www.lse.ac.uk/LSEHea
per.pdf.

Kanavos, Panos and Stacey Kowa serve the objectives of cost contr 26.
http://www.lse.ac.uk/LSEHealthAnd
N2/Kanavos%20and%20Kowal.pdf.

Kanavos, Panos, Willemien Schurer, pharmaceutical distribution chain in the impact on pharmaceutical prices". Final R Brussels, 2011.
http://eprints.lse.ac.uk/51051/1/Kanavos_pha
chain_2007.pdf.

Kanavos, Panos and Sotiris Vandoros. "Competiti Markets: Is Parallel Trade the Answer?". *Man Economics* 31, no. 5 (2010): 325-338.
https://EconPapers.repec.org/RePEc:wly:mgtdec:v:
-338.

Karanikolos, Marina, Philipa Mladovsky, Jonathan Thomson, Sanjay Basu, David Stuckler, and Johan "Financial crisis austerity, and health in Europe". *The L* 9874 (April 13): 1323-1331.
https://doi.org/10.1016/S0140-6736(13)60102-6.

Keating, Dave. "The EU's Healthy Intervention". *Europe* October 4, 2013.
https://www.politico.eu/article/the-eus-healthy-intervention/.

Kim, James H. and Anthony R. Scialli. "Thalidomide: The Trag Birth Defects and the Effective Treatment of Disease". *Toxicolo Sciences* 122, no. 1 (February 2011):1-6.

Kleijnen, Sarah, Elisabeth George, Scott Goulden, Anne d'Andon, Pauli Vitré, Boguslawa Osińska, Rafal Rdzany et al. "Relative Effectivenes Assessment of Pharmaceuticals: Similarities and Differences in 29 Jurisdictions". *Value in Health* 15, no. 6 (September – October 2012): 954-960. https://doi.org/10.1016/j.jval.2012.04.010.

Klein, Alana. "Judging as Nudging: New Governance Approaches for the Enforcement of Constitutional Social and Economic Rights". *Columbia Human Rights Law Review* 38, no. 2 (Spring 2008): 351-422.

Kristensen, Finn Børlum. "Development of European HTA: from Vision to EUnetHTA". Michael Quarterly 9 (2012): 147-156.

Permanand, Govin, and Christa Altenstetter. 'The Politics of Pharmaceuticals in the European Union'. In *Regulating Pharmaceuticals in Europe: Striving for Efficiency, Equity and Quality,* edited by Elias Mossialos, Monique Mrazek and Tom Walley, 38-54. Maidenhead: Open University Press, 2004.

Petrini, Carlo. "Regulation (EU) No. 536/2014 on clinical trials on medicinal products for human use: an overview". *Annali dell'Istituto Superiore di Sanità* 50, no. 4 (2014): 317-321. http://old.iss.it/publ/anna/2014/4/504317.pdf.

Pilgerstorfer, Marcus. "EU Law and Policy on Pharmaceuticals Marketing and Post-market Control Including Product Liability". In *Research Handbook on EU Health Law and Policy,* edited by Tamara K. Hervey, Calum Alasdair Young and Louise E. Bishop, 156-196. Cheltenham: Edward Elgar Publishing, 2017.

Porter, Michael E. "What Is Value in Health Care?". *The New England Journal of Medicine* 363, no. 26 (December 23, 2010): 2477-2481. https://doi.org/10.1056/NEJMp1011024.

Rémuzat, Cécile, Duccio Urbinati, Olfa Mzoughi, Emna El Hammi, Wael Belgaied, and Mondher Toumi. "Overview of external reference pricing systems in Europe". *Journal of Market Access & Health Policy* 3, no. 1 (September 2015): 1-11. https://doi.org/10.3402/jmahp.v3.27675.

Rieder, Clemens M. "Courts and EU health law and policies". In *Research Handbook on EU Health Law and Policy,* edited by Tamara K. Hervey, Calum Alasdair Young and Louise E. Bishop, 60-81. Cheltenham: Edward Elgar Publishing, 2017.

Santoro, Aniello, Georgy Genov, Almath Spooner, June Raine, and Peter Arlett. "Promoting and Protecting Public Health: How the European Union Pharmacovigilance System Works". *Drug Safety* 40, no. 10 (October 2017): 855-869. https://doi.org/10.1007/s40264-017-0572-8.

Savonitto, Stefano, Teresa Coppola, Paola Braglia, and Alfonso Ciccone. "Il consenso informato alla sperimentazione clinica nel paziente critico. Introduzione al Regolamento UE n. 536/2014 sulla sperimentazione clinica di medicinali per uso umano che abroga la Direttiva 2001/20/EC". *Giornale Italiano di Cardiologia* 17, no. 5 (May 2016): 326-334.

Sauter, Wolf and Johan W. Van de Gronden. "State Aid, Services of General Economic Interest and Universal Service in Healthcare". *European Competition Law Review* 32, no. 12 (January 2011): 615-620.

Scharpf, Fritz W. "The European Social Model: Coping with Challenges of Diversity". *Journal of Common Market Studies* 40, no. 4 (December 2002): 645-670.

Scholz, Nicole. *Medicinal products in the European Union: The legal framework for medicines for human use*. European Parliamentary Research Service, 2015.

Sokol, Tomislav and Nikola Mijatović. "EU Health Law and Policy and the Eurozone crisis". In *Research Handbook on EU Health Law and Policy,* edited by Tamara K. Hervey, Calum Alasdair Young and Louise E. Bishop, 291-314. Cheltenham: Edward Elgar Publishing, 2017.

Sorenson, Corinna, Michael Drummond, and Panos Kanavos. *Ensuring value for money in health care: the role of health technology assessment in the European Union*. Copenhagen: European Observatory on Health Systems and Policies, 2008.

Steichele, C., V. Abshagen, and J. Koch-Weser. *Drugs between Research and Regulations: Proceedings of the 5th International Meeting of Pharmaceutical Physicians Munich.* Berlin: Springer-Verlag Berlin Heidelberg, 2013.

Szymanski, Stefan, Tommaso Valletti, and Gabrielle Demange. "Parallel Trade, Price Discrimination, Investment and Price Caps". *Economic Policy* 20, no. 44 (October 2005): 705-749. http://www.jstor.org/stable/3601057.

Timur, Aysegul, and Gabriel Picone. "Regulating The Pharmaceutical Industry in The European Union: A Dilemma Of Achieving A Single Market". *International Business & Economics Research Journal* 8, no. 7 (December 2010): 29-42.

Torbica, Aleksandra, Rosanna Tarricone, and Michael Drummond. "Does the approach to economic evaluation in health care depend on culture, values, and institutional context?". *The European Journal of Health Economics* 19, no. 6 (July 2018): 769-774. https://doi.org/10.1007/s10198-017-0943-1.

Toumi, Mondher, Cécile Rémuzat, Anne-Lise Vataire, and Duccio Urbinati. *External reference pricing of medicinal products: simulation-based considerations for cross-country coordination. Final report*. Brussels: European Commission, 2014. https://ec.europa.eu/health/sites/health/files/healthcare/docs/erp_reimbursement_medicinal_products_en.pdf.

Valverde, Jose Luis and Paul Weissenberg. *The Challenges of the New EU Pharmaceutical Legislation.* Amsterdam: IOS press, 2005.

Van de Gronden, Johan W., and Catalin S. Rusu. "EU competition law and policy and health systems". In *Research Handbook on EU Health Law and Policy,* edited by Tamara K. Hervey, Calum Alasdair Young and Louise E. Bishop, 267-290. Cheltenham: Edward Elgar Publishing, 2017.

Vandoros, Sotiris and Tom Stargardt. "Reforms in the Greek pharmaceutical market during the financial crisis". *Health Policy* 109, no. 1 (January 2013): 1-6. https://doi.org/10.1016/j.healthpol.2012.08.016.

Velasco-Garrido, Marcial and Reinhard Busse. "Health Technology Assessment: An introduction to objectives, role of evidence, and structure in Europe". Policy Brief, European Observatory on Health Systems and Policies, 2005.

Vollaard, Hans, Hester Van de Bovenkamp and Dorte Sindbjerg Martisen. "The Making of a European Healthcare Union: A Federalist Perspective". *Journal of European Public Policy* 23, no. 2 (April 2016): 157-176.

Von Schwerun, Alexander, Heiko Stoff, and Bettina Wahrig. *Biologics, a history of agents made from living organisms in the twentieth century.* London: Routledge, 2015.

West, Peter and James Mahon. *Benefits to Payers and Patients From Parallel Trade*. York: York Health Economics Consortium, 2003.

World Medical Association. *Declaration of Helsinki – ethical principles for medical research involving human subjects*. June 1964. https://www.wma.net/policies-post/wma-declaration-of-helsinki-ethical-principles-for-medical-research-involving-human-subjects/.

INDEX